Starting with Character

Starting with Character

Activities for Infants, Toddlers, and Twos

Cathy Waggoner and Martha Herndon

Redleaf Press®
www.redleafpress.org
800-423-8309

Published by Redleaf Press
10 Yorkton Court
St. Paul, MN 55117
www.redleafpress.org

First edition 2016
Cover design by Jim Handrigan
Cover photograph by junial/Thinkstock
Interior design by Percolator
Typeset in Sirba
Printed in the United States of America
22 21 20 19 18 17 16 15   1 2 3 4 5 6 7 8

Library of Congress Cataloging-in-Publication Data
Waggoner, Cathy.
 Starting with character : activities for infants, toddlers, and twos / Cathy Waggoner and Martha Herndon. — First edition.
    pages cm
  ISBN 978-1-60554-447-2 (paperback)
1. Moral education (Preschool) 2. Character—Study and teaching—Activity programs.
3. Children—Conduct of life. I. Herndon, Martha. II. Title.
 LC268.W28 2016
 370.11'4—dc23
                       2015015852

Printed on acid-free paper

Dedication

Sometimes seeing a new generation can spark someone's vision to invest in a bold and hopeful idea. Observing the exemplary early childhood education program attended by his grandchildren, retired businessperson Robert Kirkland became inspired to help less fortunate children in his home community. Kirkland believed that at-risk children would be better equipped for school success, and become better citizens in the future, if they had opportunities to participate in high-quality early education environments similar to the one experienced by his grandchildren.

The program Kirkland's grandchildren attended used state and national standards for early learning. It was based on the philosophy that children learn best when they are in nurturing environments that are responsive to their academic- and character-development needs. Kirkland returned to his rural hometown and enlisted the help of his Rotary colleagues and several early childhood professionals. As an entrepreneurial businessperson with forty years' experience in developing successful businesses from the ground up, Kirkland applied his expertise to improving the quality of early childhood environments and school preparation experiences of the children in his community.

Kirkland's vision and generosity resulted in the creation of the nonprofit Promethean Foundation. In December 2004 the foundation began providing funds for at-risk children birth to age five to attend high-quality child care environments. Our community is forever indebted to the Kirkland family and the Robert E. and Jenny D. Kirkland Foundation for its generosity. To you we dedicate this book.

Mr. Robert E. Kirkland passed away on April 11, 2015. He was the original motivation behind the development of *Starting with Character*. He believed the teaching of good character should be intentional and by design. His spirit and character live on through the lives of those he touched.

Contents

Acknowledgments

Writing a book is not something that happens without the support and assistance of many people. When the Promethean board of directors challenged us to create a guide for teaching positive character development, it seemed at first an impossible task. The journey from research to results took years. This project would never have happened without philanthropists Robert and Jenny Kirkland and their generous Kirkland Foundation. We are also deeply grateful for the guidance of the Union City Rotary Club and governing board, the Promethean board of directors, and early childhood teachers, directors, support personnel, and community leaders.

The Kirkland Foundation charged us with the task of developing a program to teach positive character traits to children beginning at birth. We approached the task with hope and a belief in the positive outcome of our endeavors. Many people helped us in our efforts to identify and develop effective and engaging activities for infants and toddlers. As we developed ideas, we asked teachers to test them in child care centers, and we followed the children in those centers to see if the character education made a difference. We appreciate the assistance of the staff and faculty of Union City School System and Obion County School System as they continue to cooperate with us every year to collect information that helps us understand and evaluate our effectiveness. The individual teachers in the school systems we contacted were always helpful and professional in their responses. The Tennessee Department of Education offered cooperation and a listening ear. The University of Tennessee at Martin provided expertise and assistance in data analysis and volunteers for various activities. To all of you, we are thankful you were willing to participate in this manner.

We are also grateful to the staff, volunteers, and interns who worked in our office through the years helping us with data collection, data entry, daily office operation, and numerous other tasks. We appreciated your servant attitude more than you can ever know. It was a constant reminder of the good character virtues we aim to teach young children.

We want to specifically recognize some very special individual teachers for their assistance in developing activities for young children. These teachers provided valuable insights into the activities included in the book by testing them in their classrooms and contributing additional ideas. We thank them for this contribution. They include Beth Payne, teacher at Children's Corner, 2009; Joni Southerland, teacher at Kare Bear, 2009; Teena Lairy Jarmon, teacher at Pumpkin Patch, 2009; Zula Massengill, teacher at Small World, 2009; and Karen Vise, teacher at Small World, 2010.

Introduction

Starting with Character came into being when we were challenged to plan a character education program for children ages six weeks to five years. Reviewing the existing literature and resources on character education, we found very little targeting young children. Many materials designed for middle childhood and adolescence were available, but these clearly did not meet the unique and specific needs of young children. Since we know that early childhood is a critical time for learning, the lack of resources was disappointing. When we could not find a character education program for young children, we decided to create one.

Have you ever played a game of give and take with an infant? It is a wonderful experience! A baby holding a toy reaches out to hand it to you, offering it with intensity. You take the toy and say, "Thank you!" Then, after a moment of admiring the toy, you offer it back. The baby is thrilled to receive the toy and smiles! Sometimes children will repeat this activity several times. This experience demonstrates the readiness of very young children to express generosity and gratitude, positive character traits. The potential of developing character begins early; therefore, parents, caregivers, and teachers need resources to use with children starting at birth.

Research supports that the first five years represent the most critical time for brain development in children. Environmental factors contribute significantly to brain development during that time (Shore 1997). Stimulating, rich, and developmentally appropriate environments can have powerful and positive impacts, especially for at-risk children. Children's environments in the early years include their homes, the homes of friends and relatives, and their child care settings. For many, as much as 50 percent of each day is spent in child care. With this understanding, we made an effort to develop character education activities that could be integrated into high-quality early childhood environments for young children.

We all want the best for our children. We want them to grow up and be able to get along with others and to be successful in school and in their careers. We ask ourselves what success looks like. It's clear that success is more than simply learning reading, writing, and arithmetic. Success encompasses all aspects of development—mental, emotional, physical, and social. In addition, success relates to the character of a person. Therefore, integrating a focus on character development in early education makes sense. All children should have the opportunity to be successful, to be prepared for school, and to develop positive character traits.

Our book *Starting with Character: Activities for Infants, Toddlers, and Twos* became a reality through a ten-year process. Having realized the need, we set out to identify and develop activities for young children that would lay the foundation for positive character building. We hosted professional development workshops to share the results we were finding and the activities we had developed with child care providers. These providers then took the activities back to their programs and contributed feedback to us that helped further revise and develop additional activities. Eventually we decided to develop this book as a means of sharing our ideas with a broader audience.

The first four chapters of *Starting with Character* provide background information about character development in young children. The first chapter focuses on the fundamental meaning and importance of character. It also introduces the specific character traits we chose as "doable" with younger children. Chapter 2 contains information about the development of character in young children. Chapter 3 includes the strategies parents and caregivers can use to encourage positive character, and chapter 4 focuses on the importance of play and supportive environments in character development. It also includes a list of the codes used to designate specific character benefits and objectives to use with the activities that follow. The remaining chapters consist of activities: chapter 5 targets babies through fifteen months; chapter 6, toddlers; and chapter 7, two-year-olds. At the end of the book, we provide an alphabetical listing of activities by chapter, a complete bibliography of the children's literature we have highlighted, and a reference list of sources. We hope the resources in this book are as beneficial to you as they have been to us and to those who have used these activities in our community.

What Is Good Character?

Two-year-old Becky had just become a big sister to new baby William. When she heard her new brother crying on his first afternoon at home, Becky ran to her room, grabbed her favorite stuffed animal, and brought it back to him. She obviously wanted to help and thought of sharing with him her own most precious, comforting object.

Young children often amaze us by the caring and generosity they show. At other times, we know that they can be incredibly unaware of others' needs and feelings, and selfish in their reactions and behaviors. Becky, the same child who so lovingly shared her beloved toy with her new brother, later that day took a crayon and "wrote" his name on his dresser. When her mom questioned how the red marks got there, Becky rolled her eyes in her brother's direction and answered sharply, "That baby did it." Within a day's time, the same child demonstrated both unmistakable caring and seemingly spiteful dishonesty.

As caregivers, we undoubtedly find ourselves observing the behaviors of children in our lives on a daily, if not constant, basis. We notice, feel concerned, and probably step up to reprimand when the behaviors are what we consider bad or hurtful. Alternatively, we may rejoice inwardly, feel pride, and praise children when we see positive, generous, or kind behaviors. We're attuned to children's behaviors in large part because it's our job as caregivers to monitor and safeguard them. But most of us also watch and notice behaviors, looking for signs of each child's inner character. We hope to see evidence of a strong and good character emerging. And we may fear and worry about any hints of less-than-fine character in a child. We look for signs of character as we naturally wonder and ponder about what kind of adult this girl or that boy will become, what she will stand up for, or what kind of contribution he will someday make to his community.

Before going further, it will help to clarify exactly what is meant by this concept of *character*. It is one of those ideas that most likely we all understand intuitively but may never have had to define. Clearly, there are many definitions out there in the world, including statements as simple as "what a person is on the inside." For the purposes of this book, *character* is defined as *the moral and interpersonal qualities that form the essence of a person, guiding his or her behavior especially in relation to others and community*. And just as we can find numerous definitions of the concept, we can also find countless lists of qualities considered to constitute *good* character. Just a few examples are kindness, trustworthiness, fairness, courage, loyalty, and generosity.

Character is what makes each of us who we are. Our behaviors manifest our character, but character is truly more fundamental than behaviors. The word itself derives from the Greek *charakter*, referring to a stamping tool or a mark impressed or engraved on a coin. We might say that our character is something engraved on us. It is the inner compass that guides our thinking and our actions in all aspects of our lives. That is not to say that people of good character will never hurt or offend others or make poor choices; rather, the overall pattern of behavior is typically consistent with their character, no matter the circumstances.

Much has been written and hypothesized on the question of how one's character forms. We can find various theories, for example, on the role of nature or nurture. The next chapter provides a very brief overview of some of the research related to character development in young children. Suffice it to say, we believe that every person has the capability of developing, practicing, and possessing good character. The development of good character can begin and be supported in the youngest of children, even infants.

Although caregivers of infants, toddlers, and twos may sometimes find it hard to believe, these little ones are learning and forming impressions from the moment they are born. For example, research has shown that newborns recognize and can demonstrate preference for their mother's voices within days of birth (DeCasper and Fifer 1980). Researchers measured the strength and pattern of infant pacifier sucking and found that they could control and alter their sucking to trigger recordings of their own mothers' voices more often than recordings of unknown females. We also know that infants are capable of imitating simple adult facial gestures (Meltzoff and Moore 1983). In other words, learning and development begin without any formalized plan, whether caregivers are ready or not!

Of course children learn and develop cognitively and physically during their first years, but they also clearly and steadily develop in the social-emotional realm. For example, infant smiling begins at around four to six weeks, typically sparked by positive interactions with the significant people around them. Parents and caregivers of infants know very well the joy of seeing those early smiles and the fun of using tickling, baby talk, and facial expressions to encourage their frequent occurrence. It is within the context of infants earliest social-emotional developments—learning to experience, manage, and understand emotions and then relate to and interact with others—that character begins to form.

Character Develops through Interactions

Beginning at birth, interactions are the medium for all character development. Young children are shaped and influenced in fundamental ways by the quality of interactions they experience with the key adults in their lives. For example, when infants are treated with patience and gentleness by caregivers, they begin to absorb and instinctively appreciate those qualities in human interactions. When infants cry and their needs are met, they begin to build a foundation of trust in their caregivers. The ability to trust others helps build positive connections and supports their instinct to then be trustworthy themselves in the future. Long before children can cognitively understand or describe the qualities of good character, they can intuitively and emotionally sense and appreciate the feelings associated with those qualities.

Although parents and other family members in the home are the major influence on children's character development, all caregivers and teachers who interact with them can make a difference. Caregivers can support an infant's character development by meeting her needs for cuddling, feeding, diapering, and social interaction in consistently loving and respectful ways during the span of time the infant is in their care. Likewise, caregivers can support a toddler's and a two-year-old's character development through rich conversations and play, role modeling, and consistently respectful treatment.

Caregivers and parents are encouraged to realize their potential to guide young children in character development right from the start. We don't have to wait until children can speak, read, or understand sophisticated intellectual concepts to begin teaching character. There are endless opportunities to teach and support the development of good character in very young children. Clearly the best approach for doing so is by setting a good example. When children see their significant adults exhibiting positive character traits, they internalize those traits and often imitate the behaviors. Picture fifteen-month-old Tamika watching her mom gently helping her aging Granny settle into a chair. Tamika then goes up and pats Granny on the knee. She is clearly imitating a gesture she saw her mom previously perform to comfort Granny. Or imagine eighteen-month-old Jacob watching his caregiver comfort baby Gina after her parent leaves. Jacob then goes to crying Gina and hands her a toy to play with, imitating a comforting gesture he has witnessed or experienced.

Although one's character is more fundamental than simply one's behaviors, there is great value in simply teaching and expecting the behaviors that exemplify good character, even when children are too young to truly comprehend explanations of or rationale for the behaviors. In fact, there can be a synergistic relationship between practicing actions associated with positive character and gradual development of the associated character trait. For example, when parents expect children to say thank you upon receiving a gift, children may not yet truly understand gratitude but are practicing the behavior.

Be Sensitive to Developmental Stages

When supporting the development of good character, it is important for parents and caregivers to be attuned to the normal and appropriate developmental stages through which children pass. Such sensitivity can help adults convey character messages in developmentally appropriate ways. It can also assuage concerns about a child's "bad" or challenging behaviors that may in fact be perfectly normal for their developmental stage and not at all reflective of poor character. For example, little Becky's instinct to accuse her baby brother of her wrongdoing in the earlier story was a natural outcome of her two-year-old inability to process the major emotional upheaval that occurs when a new baby arrives. Think about toddlers who routinely grab toys from other children. In the vast majority of cases, this behavior doesn't indicate poor character; rather, it is a normal developmental stage in which sharing is challenging. Toddlers naturally focus on their own needs and wants at the exclusion of others.

While we often talk about children's development as if it can be separated into parts, such as social-emotional, physical, language, or cognitive, the fact is that children's development is a total package. Character development is interdependent with all other areas of development. Consequently, any effort to "teach" or support character development should be appropriately matched with developmental expectations. In doing so, the character lessons can contribute to building important foundations for learning. For example, we know that young children learn best through play. So verbally explaining the importance of sharing will be far less effective than instigating playful games that allow children to practice sharing while having fun.

Be Patient

Perhaps it goes without saying that teaching good character is not like teaching a specific cognitive or physical skill, in which an outcome or accomplishment can be clearly assessed. Character formation is cumulative, gradual, and may be largely unobservable during the early years. Just as children pass from one developmental stage to another, with each accomplishment building a foundation for the next, one experience or impression of positive character can be the building block for the next. Although a two-year-old may not voluntarily share her toys, it doesn't mean that there is no value in letting her observe sharing, as well as encouraging and inviting her to try, though it may be very challenging at first. We can help her to gradually view sharing in a new way, as interesting and potentially fun, even if it might be a little scary. Suddenly one day we will turn around, and she will be sharing on her own. A caregiver or parent can never know exactly when the seeds she plants will germinate and begin to grow into legitimately self-motivated acts on the part of the child.

Character Traits to Support in Young Children

The youngest years are prime for character development, and yet in our experience as early childhood professionals, we have found that much of the discussion and literature on character and character building focuses on older children and adults, assuming a certain cognitive ability and communication skill level. There are few materials or resources for supporting character development in infants, toddlers, and twos.

This book provides everyday interactions and play activities that caregivers and parents can do with infants, toddlers, and twos that serve to promote character development. Some of these activities may be familiar to you, although you may not have thought about how they can also serve to stimulate good character qualities. Focusing on this potential benefit can help us better appreciate our influence as caregivers on young children and inspire us to be more intentional in our interactions.

As mentioned, one could list many qualities commonly associated with good character. In this book, we focus on six that can truly be supported, modeled, demonstrated, and encouraged to manifest during the earliest years: caring, honesty, integrity, respect, responsibility, and self-discipline. These six traits are also commonly found in other literature on character development.

Caring

The ability to show caring is a pillar of good character. There are benefits to creating a world where people freely demonstrate caring. We would all be healthier and happier if we cared consistently for others, the environment, and ourselves. In a caring world, children would be nurtured (not neglected or abused), adults would demonstrate their care for one another, homes would be comfortable and inviting, and people would be safe and have access to fundamental services and comforts.

Infants and young children intuitively yearn to be comforted and cared for by loving adults. Perhaps even more importantly, they are entirely dependent on adults' care. Therefore, they are constantly learning and observing, through the type of care they receive, what it means to care for another. This happens long before they can cognitively process or describe the actions of caring. Like Becky in the opening story, very young children often demonstrate caring behaviors possibly driven by instinct, or maybe modeled after what they have experienced or observed in the past. Regardless, the expression of caring is one that can be easily affirmed, supported, and encouraged in very young children.

As children grow physically and cognitively, they can begin practicing simple caring behaviors, such as gentle touches toward pets and friends, careful handling of toys and belongings, respectful treatment of flowers and nature, and regular hand washing and bathing. Very young children can also observe and mimic in a rudimentary fashion how the adults in their lives care for themselves, including personal safety, health, hygiene, nutrition, and appearance. Describing self-care actions to young children is powerful even if they don't fully understand the words, and it can begin to build their caring vocabulary. For example, before meals we can demonstrate and describe hand washing by saying, "I need to wash my hands before I eat to get rid of all the germs. I'll use soap and scrub, scrub, scrub until they are clean."

An ethic of caring for the environment can also begin forming in the first years. As adults we can intentionally pick up trash or maintain a backyard bird feeder and describe what we're doing to children. We can care for our indoor environments by keeping them clean and arranging them aesthetically and efficiently. Intentional room arrangements with clear and accessible storage for toys can help toddlers and twos learn to care for their things. When we encourage children to pick up their own toys, feed the pets, pick up trash, turn off the water spigot after using, and handle flowers gently, they experience basic but valuable lessons in caring for the environment, our shared space.

Honesty

Honesty is the basis for trust and a critical ingredient in loving, fulfilling, successful relationships. Not only do we want and need to trust other people in order to function successfully in society, but we also want and need others to trust us.

The foundation for understanding and embracing trust and honesty begins in infancy through children's experience of the care they receive by their significant adults. Children begin learning to trust when they experience consistent and predictable nurturing care. Long before they can define or explain their feelings, children develop instincts about others' trustworthiness. Experiencing others to be trustworthy fuels children's instinct to then be trustworthy themselves.

Young children continue to develop their understanding of honesty through their experiences with pretend play. Through this type of play, they get valuable practice in distinguishing between what is real and what is not real. At a certain developmental stage, it is perfectly normal for toddlers to get somewhat confused about this distinction and perhaps seem to devote far more energy to the imaginary world than the real. But this is not something to worry about. The imagination is a critical cognitive tool that will serve them in countless ways as they mature, including helping them understand others' perspectives, visualize and solve problems, come up with new ideas, and think creatively. Ultimately their experiences in pretend play will help to clarify the distinction between real and pretend, and to develop their ability to grasp the reality of truth.

At a certain stage, it is also common for young children to make up stories as a way of explaining things they do not understand or to avoid punishment, as in the earlier scenario with big sister Becky. This is developmentally normal and not an indication of dishonest character. Adults can promote honesty by giving gentle feedback, helping children to distinguish between truth and fiction, and embracing the truth even when it is challenging.

Beginning from birth, children benefit from seeing us model honesty in our relationships. This sounds like a simple task, but it can be challenging. We may often lie to children without thinking. For example, a parent may say, "Mmm . . . this medicine is good," as a way of encouraging the child to take it. When the child swallows the medicine and finds it to be horribly bitter, she experiences a parent who didn't tell the truth. It would be better to say something like, "Medicine will make you feel better." Other times, we may say, "You're not hurt," when we want to encourage a child to recover from a fall quickly without inconveniencing us, while in fact the child definitely feels pain. Failing to acknowledge a child's legitimate feelings is a form of dishonesty. It would be better to say, "I know falling hurts, but let me help you stand so I can check your hurt."

Another example of mild, yet significant, parental dishonesty is when parents sneak away from home or child care drop-off without saying good-bye because they wish to avoid a tearful and challenging scene. This is an understandable choice, as it is not easy to deal with an upset and clingy child. But what message does it communicate to the child? It is better to face the departure with honesty and help children learn to accept the process of separation. Children honestly need to know what we expect from them and what they can expect from us.

Integrity

Related to honesty, integrity is the quality of having strong moral principles and values that guide one's decisions and actions regardless of circumstances. People with high integrity make decisions consistently in line with their values and do what they say they will do, opting not to cut corners or slough off responsibilities even when they might face an easy opportunity to do so without penalty or consequence.

Young children form their first unconscious impressions of integrity through observing the behaviors of parents, caregivers, and teachers. Adults demonstrate integrity in small but significant ways when we do things like stop consistently at stop signs, even when no one is watching, or walk the extra few steps to place the soda can in the recycling bin rather than the more convenient trash can.

We can support children in their development of integrity by starting early with providing them opportunities to practice simple decision making. Decision making empowers children by giving them a sense of control. It also lets them gradually develop awareness of their reasons for making a certain choice, not to mention the consequences that any given choice might have. For example, if you choose to play at the water table, your sleeves will most likely get wet. If you flip the lunch plate upside down, your food gets mangled and mixed up. When children make "good" choices, caregivers can reinforce their choice by praising them and verbally noting the positive consequences. When they make "bad" choices, caregivers can let them experience the negative consequences, including our disapproval. Some young children will be highly motivated by the desire for an adult's approval but, given time and experience, will eventually mature into finding inner motivation for doing what is right.

Adults can also encourage children's development of integrity by supporting them in following through with decisions. Follow-through sometimes takes great courage, especially when it involves doing something that is new or challenging, such as climbing the big slide for the first time or experimenting with dipping their face into water in the baby pool. Children gain courage to follow through on decisions by having support and encouragement from loving caregivers. At times this kind of support might involve shadowing a young child in order to physically help him follow through on a decision. At other times it may be as simple as staying nearby, ready to help if the situation should require it.

Respect

Respect is an attitude of honoring parents, others, nature, beliefs, property, and self, and it is key to well-being and healthy relationships. When people treat others with respect, they work to see others' points of view and care for their feelings, and they exhibit courtesy and polite manners in their interactions. Although we often think of respect as something demonstrated between peers or shown by young people toward elders, adults can and should show respect to young children, thereby demonstrating it and helping them embrace it for themselves.

Parents, caregivers, and teachers can show respect for infants by caring for them consistently, with patience and gentleness. Toddlers and two-year-olds can be shown respect by acknowledging each child's presence and individuality, treating each as a highly valued individual, listening attentively to every child's communications, and responding sensitively to their needs and feelings. Young children notice and value when they are treated with respect. They yearn to be noticed positively, acknowledged for their skills and abilities, and allowed to proceed independently.

Listening well is an obvious way of demonstrating respect for others and is especially powerful when adults listen well and attentively to young children. Starting from a very young age, children notice when adults give them their full attention or conversely give only partial or distracted attention. This does not mean that we should grant children our undivided attention every single time they ask for it. Children also benefit greatly from learning to wait patiently for "their turn" to receive attention while adults engage in business or conversation. Such experiences of appropriate waiting provide important lessons in respect.

We can demonstrate and teach children respect for others through practicing good manners, such as covering our mouths when we cough or saying "Excuse me" when we bump into someone. It's our job as caregivers to remind children of good manners, review and help them practice the skills, and then praise them when they successfully remember to use manners without a reminder.

When children exhibit behavior that we perceive as disrespectful, we have an opportunity to teach about respect. We may feel angry, but we can turn situations around by modeling respect and giving children the vocabulary and actions they need to communicate respect in return. For example, when a child makes the demand "Gimme juice," we can respond by simply and respectfully stating that we expect her to use polite words at the table, and wait until she says or signs "please" before giving her the juice.

Responsibility

Responsibility is the state of being personally accountable for and trusted to accomplish something. Most people vividly remember the exciting moments of being entrusted with our first adult responsibilities—perhaps being allowed to take the family car or accepting a first paying job or receiving a promotion to a management position. We recall how much pride and excitement we felt to know that we were trusted and deemed worthy of such responsibilities. Being granted responsibility often fuels one to feel more capable and to strive to excel or grow in one's abilities.

In the same way, children can experience a level of excitement and pride when they are given responsibility for age-appropriate tasks and chores. The seeds of accepting and embracing responsibility are planted in the first years through having opportunities to carry out simple, developmentally appropriate tasks. A baby can be given the simple task of holding a clean diaper while being changed. A one-year-old can have the job of hanging his coat on a child-height peg. By age two, children can be assigned very simple chores, like helping to pick up toys, feeding pets, and putting dirty clothes into hampers.

Just like adults, young children experience great satisfaction and pride in completing jobs. Children also experience a sense of being "in control" and a measure of independence, an extremely positive experience for toddlers and twos. Yes, an adult can do the job faster and much more efficiently, but if we constantly do everything for children, they miss opportunities to develop their own sense of responsibility. As young children get older, they benefit greatly from experiencing gradual increases in responsibility.

Self-Discipline

Self-discipline is the ability to control one's behavior, respect rules, pursue and achieve goals, stick with difficult challenges, resist problematic temptations, and make good decisions. It is key to both individual success and a smoothly functioning society.

Self-discipline is an extremely important developmental skill for children, enabling successes for them just as much as it does for adults. Young children need self-discipline to develop physically, control their bodies, and manage basic emotions and urges. Adults can support infants in the development of self-discipline by providing secure, loving care and environments where they can experience feelings of safety and self-worth. Feeling safe and valuable frees the brain to focus on growth.

We can support toddlers and twos by providing clear rules, limits, and expectations. Children yearn for the structure and safety of clear expectations. We can also guide children in developing self-discipline by suggesting strategies and creating situations that facilitate their successes. For example, young children are often tantalized by electronic devices, such as phones and computers. We can make an effort to keep these devices out of their sight, thus limiting a very difficult temptation, and we can make more appropriate toys available to engage them.

Caregivers can also intervene as necessary when children are struggling or unable to control their behavior. If we see a toddler is about to knock all the toys off the shelf, we can step in to redirect her attention toward more constructive behaviors. We can also praise children and provide plenty of positive feedback when they do exhibit self-control.

Perhaps above all else, we can role-model self-discipline in the daily choices and activities with which we engage. Self-discipline is not typically achieved in a once-and-for-all manner. It is more often a practice to which we all must dedicate and rededicate ourselves throughout our lives. Experiencing early lessons and successes in self-discipline can create momentum for the practice in adulthood.

Why Teach Good Character?

We support character development in children because we want to help them be successful in the world, and we know that having fine, upstanding character will help them toward that goal. We also want to raise children who will contribute to a better future and a healthy world. The lessons of good character are at the core of creating a better place for all of us to live. Our world would continue to improve if all people were more respectful and caring, honest and responsible, and dedicated to making good choices. We can't necessarily change the world, but we can change one small piece—our interactions with the young children in our care. We can help guide children to develop positive character traits from the beginning by intentionally exposing them to the values and qualities we consider important. We can begin by making these lessons key for children. Caregivers can make a significant difference in promoting children's success in life.

In Conclusion

Each home, classroom, and community should be a place where people feel safe and secure, able to express themselves as individuals, and confident in the underlying and consistent set of positive values that shape rules and interactions. Parents are a child's first teachers, but we are all part of a network influencing the social and cultural environments of young children. Teaching character is the responsibility of parents, grandparents, caregivers, teachers, and the community. We are partners working together to support children as they learn the vital lessons necessary to contribute to a just and caring society.

It's important, therefore, to intentionally build character lessons into the daily activities of family life and child care rather than leaving them to chance. Planning for good character changes children by promoting a positive social environment. This book contains ideas to use in teaching good character, including suggestions for incorporating character lessons in language, reading, math, science, social studies, music, and art. When we integrate good character into everything we teach, it becomes a part of all learning.

2

 ## Character Development in the First Three Years

The period from infancy through age three is an important window in which children form key relationships and begin to understand and develop character traits. Positive traits can and should be taught and supported in children during those years. Historically there has been a widespread belief that infants, toddlers, and two-year-olds aren't ready for character lessons because they have limited language abilities and have not yet developed the capacity to understand others' perspectives. Thus most materials on teaching character have been designed for older children. Yet it has become clear that tremendous social-emotional development takes place during the first three years. Very young children are highly socially responsive and primed to learn through social interactions. For parents, caregivers, and teachers, that means we have uniquely rich opportunities for influencing them in the formation of positive character through role modeling and through integrating positive messages and experiences into our interactions with them.

Traditional Views on Moral Development

For decades, discussion and research on early moral development did not fully acknowledge the potential in the early childhood years. The renowned Swiss psychologist Jean Piaget notably labeled young children "egocentric," unable to understand any perspective other than their own (Piaget 1932; Wadsworth 1996). Meanwhile the influential American psychologist Lawrence Kohlberg (1976) described very young children as following rules only to avoid punishment or loss of parental love; in other words, exhibiting moral behavior only in response to external forces, not internal. Feminist psychologist Carol Gilligan (1993) strongly criticized Kohlberg's theory, observing that he did not account for the significance of relationships and caring in moral development. Yet even Gilligan focused her own research and theory on the moral thinking of school-age children, adolescents, and adults rather than on infants and young children.

New Insights and Perspectives

In recent years, the long-standing theories about moral development have been revisited and questioned by numerous researchers proposing that in fact young children have significant capacity for independent moral thinking and development. This newer viewpoint is informed by in-depth research and observations of very young children interacting with their significant adults. It also springs from important developments in research methodology, such as brain imaging, that have opened up whole new windows into exploring the workings and development of young children's preverbal brains. Many researchers today argue that the fundamental building blocks of moral development absolutely begin in the first year of life through emotional experiences, social referencing, and the influence of significant relationships and personal interactions.

The Social-Emotional Potential in Infants

It was once common to think of infants as helpless, nonthinking beings, whose actions and responses were purely reflex- or sensory-driven. We now know that infants' brains are working in remarkably more complex ways, taking in information and adjusting their responses as they interact with their environment and the people around them. You may recall the study mentioned in chapter 1, which showed that infants only a few days old can recognize and demonstrate a preference for their mothers' voices by adjusting the strength and frequency of their sucking on pacifiers so as to hear recordings of their own mothers more often than recordings of unknown females.

Other research has further reinforced that infants and very young children have remarkably rich emotional capacities. Within the first six months of age, they are able to express the primary emotions, including surprise, interest, joy, anger, sadness, fear, and disgust (Lewis 2013). Experiencing these emotions provides a crucial foundation for social-emotional growth. Sometime in their second year, children begin exhibiting a range of "self-conscious" emotions, including jealousy, empathy, embarrassment, pride, shame, and guilt (Lewis 2013). These emotions are uniquely human and require one to have a fundamental base of self-awareness. By the age of three, children are typically capable of expressing the full range of human emotions.

Various studies have shown that infants are more highly aware of others and have greater capacity to interact intentionally with others than previously thought. Infants can imitate simple facial expressions (Meltzoff and Moore 1983). During the first year, they develop the ability to follow another's gaze with their eyes, which is a key step toward grasping others' perspectives as different from one's own (Brooks and Meltzoff 2005). Infants are attracted to smiling faces or face-like images, as shown by a study that documented infants looking at smiling face images far longer than nonsmiling faces (Wilcox and Clayton 1968). In yet another study involving face-to-face interactions, infants smiled more when their mothers smiled at them than when strangers smiled at them (Messinger, Fogel, and Dickson 1999). Still another study found that by five months old, infants can discriminate between different strangers' faces despite the strangers making similar expressions. Moreover, infants can discriminate between expressions of fear and happiness and comprehend different intensities of happiness as shown through multiple photos of the same person with different smiles (Bornstein and Arterberry 2003).

Researchers have also demonstrated that infants have a basic capacity for empathy, the fundamental human sense of feeling another's pain. For example, one study documented that when newborns heard the cries of other infants, they responded with crying and negative facial expressions (Dondi, Simion, and Caltran 1999). Empathy is at the heart of caring relationships and social-emotional growth. It is also essential to good character as many positive character qualities are rooted in the ability to understand and demonstrate concern for others' perspectives. People of good character can see and prioritize the greater good of community over personal self-interest.

We know that young children also have the distinct ability to read emotional cues on others' faces, which is a particularly important tool for social-emotional growth and development. The term *social referencing* refers to looking to others for emotional cues as to how one should respond to situations. Studies have found that infants look to an adult's face and adapt their response to match that of the adult, for example, becoming scared, worried, or happy (Walden and Ogan 1988; Kim and Kwak 2011). Social referencing is a crucial step in the process of developing the ability to perceive others' feelings and perspectives and understand that they are different from one's own. This is a critical interpersonal skill and component in building successful relationships. In addition, it shows that children have a degree of self-control over their own emotions, looking to a parent or caregiver before reacting.

Character Potential Grows in Toddlers and Twos

By their first birthday, children typically are well on their way toward achieving a strong self-awareness. This is an important step in character development because it fuels the basic understanding of others as separate beings with their own thoughts, feelings, and experiences. An ingenious method was used to measure young children's emerging self-awareness by placing a dot of rouge on their noses, then placing them individually in front of a mirror. If a child reached to touch his nose while looking in the mirror, he clearly realized he was looking at his own reflection. The researchers found that by twenty to twenty-four months of age, most children clearly point to the spot of rouge, indicating clear self-recognition and self-awareness (Amsterdam 1972; Lewis and Brooks-Gunn 1979).

In the second year of life, children show even more capacity to grasp and embrace qualities associated with good character. It is quite normal for one- and two-year-olds to understand and participate in positive social behaviors, such as sharing, cooperation, and helping. These "prosocial" behaviors require cognitive and emotional development as well as specific skills. Cognitively, a child must be able to see himself as separate from other individuals, understand that another person has needs, be able to use language, and have enough memory to keep the other person's need in mind. Emotionally, a child must have the ability to empathize with another and respond to that person's emotional state. Sharing and turn taking are specific skills that can be modeled and taught by parents and caregivers. Some have argued that children who have secure attachments to caregivers who consistently model prosocial behaviors have the best chance of developing these prosocial skills (Marion 1999).

Toddlers and twos love to do things for themselves and are actively pursuing a sense of autonomy (Erikson 1950). They can walk, climb, push, pull, and cause all manner of effects by their actions. They feel a sense of pride in their abilities and want to push the boundaries of what they can do. The experience of autonomy and the pride that comes from independent accomplishment are part of character formation, in particular building a basic understanding of responsibility. On the other hand, when toddlers don't have opportunities to do things for themselves and experience the pride of accomplishment, they may experience doubt or uncertainty, in some cases even shame, instead of the positive sense of autonomy that fuels good character traits.

Two-year-olds also begin to develop a sense of initiative. They can tell caregivers when they need to use the restroom and can initiate hand washing, dressing/undressing, and other basic tasks. Twos get a great deal of satisfaction from being able to follow simple steps to complete a task. A sense of initiative is a vital step in positive character development. Supporting their initiative by allowing them to pursue activities independently helps promote feelings of empowerment and confidence, fueling character development.

The Importance of Healthy Relationships in the Early Years

As mentioned in chapter 1, character is above all shaped through children's interactions with others, particularly their primary caregivers. When caregivers consistently respond to infants' needs, babies feel a sense of well-being and begin to trust that when they have needs, they will be met. Trust leads to successful relationships with other people and fuels further social-emotional growth. On the other hand, when caregivers do not respond to the needs of infants, infants learn they cannot trust their needs to be met. A child who develops mistrust in caregivers has difficulty developing close relationships and will also doubt herself, adversely affecting future self-confidence and relationships.

Children are more likely to respond positively to those with whom they have developed strong and healthy attachments, and such attachments are the basis for a positive sense of self. Mary Ainsworth (1979) studied mothers as they interacted with their infants and toddlers by observing them at home and evaluating the attachment. She concluded that a secure attachment is associated with caregivers being consistently responsive to their young children. She also argued that infants are active participants in forming attachments through such behaviors as crying, gazing, clinging, and seeking the caregiver. With secure attachments, children can grow in empathy, caring, respect, and all other traits of good character.

In Conclusion

Character development is clearly a multifaceted and gradual process with many complex factors. Several aspects have not yet been thoroughly studied or are not understood completely, although the research has made it quite clear that the seeds of character are indeed sown in the first years of life. The character traits of caring, honesty, integrity, and respect are grounded in the development of trust between young children and their caregivers. The seeds of self-discipline are sown through basic practice of problem solving and self-control. And the foundation of responsibility, not to mention many other character qualities (such as loyalty, per-severance, sacrifice, and generosity), is laid through young children's experiences in pursuing independent goals, encountering challenges, imagining solutions, coping with emotions, and relating with others in steadily more complex ways during the early childhood years.

3

 # How Can We Support Character Development in Young Children?

As previously mentioned, influencing and supporting character development in young children starts with building positive trusting relationships. Beyond fostering good character, such relationships provide a critical foundation for all learning, growth, self-confidence, and future accomplishments. The first three years are a time when young children are naturally forming attachments and seeking social cues from the adults in their lives. At the same time, they are undergoing tremendous physical, cognitive, and social-emotional growth. The combination of significant development and social receptivity makes this an ideal time for supporting and encouraging their development of positive character.

Positive relationships between children and their significant adults grow from positive, loving interactions. And those require dedicating time and energy, as well as meeting children where they are developmentally. As with any area of learning, we should not expect nor demand more than what children are ready for, yet there are countless developmentally appropriate ways to support the formation of positive character. In particular, we would like to highlight the following strategies: modeling and demonstrating the behaviors associated with good character, engaging in conversations, creating safe and secure environments, being consistent, having clear expectations, scaffolding skills, and practicing good character traits through play. This chapter describes these seven strategies, in particular how each can be effective in supporting positive character development in young children during the first three years of life.

Modeling and Demonstrating

It's all too easy to be unaware of our influence as adults on the children around us, yet they are constantly watching and observing, even when they don't seem to be. From us, they form impressions on how to talk, act, and react. Young children will pattern their behavior after our example no matter what we do. Picture a one-year-old picking up a stick and beginning to hit a tree after observing his dad hammering nails into a fence. Or there's the scenario of a toddler who picks up a toy, holds it to her ear, and begins to "talk" away as if on the phone, complete with vocal inflections shockingly similar to those of her mom or dad. Long before we think she even knows what a phone is, she shows that she has it all figured out.

Above all other strategies, we can support positive character development in children by striving to cultivate and practice the character qualities we wish them to embrace. Make a point of asking yourself, "Am I modeling something I want them to copy?" or "Am I behaving consistently with what I ask of them?" We send a mixed message when children hear us yell at a driver who cuts us off on the highway and then tell them it is not nice to yell at others or when we snack while walking around the house or child care center but tell them, "You have to sit at the table if you want to eat." As parents and caregivers, our days are full of opportunities to model positive behaviors for the children in our care. When we listen attentively as children talk to us, or patiently wipe noses and wash dirty faces, we model caring and respect. When we accept apologies graciously, we model humility, respect, and forgiveness for others who may have made a mistake. If we repeatedly model positive character traits, we will undoubtedly see our children imitating them.

Conversations

Conversations are the most common mode of interaction among people. Conversations with children can support character development by allowing us to verbally demonstrate honesty and respect, not to mention gratitude, kindness, comfort, and caring. Engaging young children in conversations can also promote language development, thereby helping them to develop their own tools for verbally exhibiting their character.

Conversations between mothers and their children begin even before birth. By around thirty weeks gestational age, a fetus can distinguish his mother's voice from others and responds to it with altered movement, heart rate, or both (DeCasper and Fifer 1980). Newborns can recognize the unique sounds of their mother's native tongue (Moon, Cooper, and Fifer 1993). This early language perception and sensitivity help babies to form strong attachments to their significant adults and launch them on their lifelong journey as social beings.

Parents and caregivers are encouraged to talk freely with young children even before the little ones have the verbal skills to respond. Albeit one-sided, such "conversations" provide invaluable exposure to respectful speaking as well as basic language and speech patterns. Babies may not understand all or any of the words we use, but we know that listening to people speak to them, in particular their mothers, activates key areas of their brains that are associated with learning. A one-sided conversation with a baby could be as simple as this: "Hello Kane, let's give you some tummy time. I'm going to lay you on this colorful blanket and give you some toys to play with." In speaking respectfully and lovingly to babies, we can provide comfort and nurturing during daily experiences, such as diapering, feeding, playing, and bathing.

As children's verbal skills develop, they will begin participating in the conversation. At first it may be only some "oohs" or "aahs." But before we know it, babies are imitating some of our sounds. Words come together, and a conversation becomes two-sided.

Toddlers and twos are putting words together to express thoughts. Their words and thoughts may be quite simple, but we can nonetheless intentionally engage them in conversation by listening attentively, responding respectfully and with interest, and asking open-ended questions to encourage focused thought and sharing.

Character development is guided by role-modeling those skills, and we also build loving relationships as well as children's self-esteem. Through conversations, parents and caregivers will occasionally be rewarded with rich nuggets of insight into a child's worldview and development, as well as be provided with opportunities to guide them. Take, for example, the following exchange between a mom and her two-year-old:

CHILD: Drew won't play, Mommy.
MOM: That's too bad. Why do you think he doesn't want to play?
CHILD: He likes my horsie.
MOM: Hmmm. Do you think maybe he feels bad when you don't let him
play with your horsie? Maybe he just wants a turn to play with it?
CHILD (*happily*): I share my horsie.

This exchange opened the door for learning about how we make friends and keep them. Young children are just beginning to develop their relationship skills, often limited by their language, and many times they need direction in how to be a friend. This mom had an important and constructive interaction with her child that could have been missed if she had not taken the time to listen to her child's conversation attempts.

Safe, Secure Environments

When young children feel safe and secure, they are more able and likely to explore and learn about the world around them. Feeling excessively scared, hungry, tired, or starved for attention causes stress and fundamental feelings of insecurity. Without a core feeling of security, children will instinctively focus on self-preservation or survival rather than growth and learning, thus limiting their opportunities for positive character development.

Stable, consistent relationships are the most important source of security for a young child. Children naturally form attachments to their primary caregivers. If the care or attention they receive is inconsistent, cold, or harsh, children feel stress and agitation, thus limiting the energy they can dedicate to growth and exploration. Consistent, loving, and respectful attention, on the other hand, helps to build a base of self-worth and security, freeing them up to pour their energy into exploration and learning.

Young children also benefit greatly from having safe and secure environments in which they can freely explore and experiment without risk of mishap or injury. Having the freedom to explore a space promotes confidence, courage, self-worth, and learning. When children are injured in an unsafe space, perhaps by falling down stairs, hitting their head on a sharp corner, or touching the hot stove, they can experience a loss of confidence and a surge of insecurity. Children can also sense when adults are anxious and fearful about their safety. On the other hand, when adults are confident that an environment is safe and thoroughly child-proofed, their confidence empowers little ones. That said, the world is inherently dangerous for infants and toddlers despite our best efforts to protect them and to childproof spaces. When they do experience pain or injury, we can reassure them with calming words and actions, conveying the message that they will be fine and can still have confidence to explore.

We must be mindful that dangers change as children develop. For example, babies need to be protected from older children, falls, and suffocating hazards. Crawlers and toddlers face the heightened risk of falling down stairs or overturning household objects or furniture as they practice their movements. Two-year-olds are just becoming independent, capable, and curious enough to be especially dangerous. They might wander out of our sight during a moment of distraction or be drawn to explore household cleaning supplies or the workings of electrical appliances. Children need constant monitoring and supervision by adults throughout the first three years as they practice the skills, actions, and activities that lead toward independence. Providing adequate supervision encourages them to pursue and accomplish challenges, fueling their growth.

Consistent Routines and Environments

Consistency in routines and environments is important for young children. Children who never know from one day to the next where they are going, or with whom, or what is going to happen next typically experience high levels of unrest and stress. Consistency relieves stress and allows children to concentrate on growth and learning. It helps children learn to trust and be open to caregivers and to deepen their attachments. It can also help them to be more open to new or unknown situations, challenging themselves to grow and learn.

Change is constant for children. They do not control the majority of their daily decisions or activities. Even their bodies are constantly changing and growing. Changes and transitions can cause them tremendous stress. Like most adults, young children cope with change more easily if they know to expect it and are not overloaded with multiple changes at once. Consistency in routines and environments can go a long way toward helping children manage the normal daily changes and allowing them to feel secure and trusting in their caregivers. Consistent routines and environments can also foster important qualities of good character, such as self-discipline and a sense of responsibility. When children have the same routines every day, they learn the steps and develop the capability to do what is expected of them by their own initiative.

Just about any daily activity can become a positive routine. For example, many families have routines around wake-up time, tooth brushing, or bedtime procedures. Of course mealtime is a natural setting for creating and practicing routines, whether it be a before-meal blessing, a certain pattern of conversation, or simply the daily act of sitting down together at the same time. Mealtime routines can easily become treasured elements of childhood, especially when they feature quality time and conversation with all the family together. Child care centers often have routines centered around arrival, departure, circle time, rest time, eating, diapering, hand washing, story time, and naptime. When working with groups of young children, routines are an especially critical tool for promoting cooperative behavior and individual self-initiative. Parents often remark to the child care professional, "How do you get all these children to take a nap at the same time?" The answer is by making it part of a consistent routine. When it's their routine, children do what is expected of them.

Transition times, which can be especially upsetting for young children, often become smoother when comforting routines are in place. For example, young children typically cooperate more readily with challenging bedtime steps, such as tooth brushing, when they are looking forward to nightly reading and snuggle time with Mom or Dad. In the child care setting, the morning drop-off can be eased by the routine of going to a certain window and waving good-bye to parents. Children look forward to the routine as they transition, and they experience a sense of control and comfort by simply having the knowledge of what is coming.

Developing routines takes time, patience, and repetition. When we attempt to introduce a new routine, it's easy to get discouraged if young children don't get it immediately. But we must keep at it. An action does not become a routine until it is done repeatedly and consistently. After a routine is learned and the expected behavior becomes second nature, children feel empowered and proud that they can predict what is going to happen.

As wonderful as routines can be, the reality is that they do get interrupted, which can be challenging for both children and adults. Sometimes we have to go with plan B. Role modeling a positive response to interruptions can help little ones develop their coping skills and build their resilience. Children accept changes more readily if we explain them with a calm voice. This strategy reassures children and provides an opportunity for meaningful communication about change. Adults can also prepare ahead of time for interruptions. Having an extra book or activity at the ready can save the day as well as help children accept that interruptions are a normal part of life.

Consistency in environments is also important, in much the same way as schedule consistency. It helps children feel secure and can foster the sense of responsibility, initiative, and self-discipline. When a two-year-old knows how the environment is arranged, where things go, and how to participate in caring for it, he feels ownership and responsibility for the space. He is more likely to help with keeping it clean and orderly because he trusts in the consistency.

Clear Expectations

Young children want to know what is expected of them. Clear expectations typically result in fewer behavioral problems. Perhaps more importantly, setting forth clear expectations fosters a sense of initiative, responsibility, and self-discipline as children begin to independently embrace appropriate behaviors. Children can then experience positive results in terms of greater potential for accomplishment and control over situations, richer connections with others, and adult approval and praise. When a toddler has a clear expectation about her bedtime, she will be more inclined to cooperate and comply with the routines. She will respond because she knows what is expected and she feels a sense of accomplishment.

We may think children automatically know what is expected of them, but their understanding is often limited by their lack of life experience or language. Expectations should be defined in simple terms, modeled, practiced, and then reinforced through reminders, firm guidance, encouragement, praise, and smiles. For example, when giving crayons to a two-year-old, we could say, "The crayons are for drawing on this paper. Show me you know where to use crayons." Meanwhile we could draw on the paper to model the appropriate behavior.

Expectations of children should of course be developmentally appropriate. We would not expect a typical toddler to sit quietly and listen to a book for thirty minutes or a one-year-old to pick up a roomful of toys. But a toddler might listen for ten minutes, and a baby might pick up one toy that is within reach and hand it to a caregiver. A toddler can understand an expectation of "no hitting" but may continue to need reminders of acceptable methods for handling confrontation with others. A two-year-old may know he is supposed to go the toilet when he feels the urge but may still get involved in play and forget to go.

Establishing clear expectations requires patience and consistency on the part of adults. Sometimes we must state or demonstrate our expectations many times before they are respected. For example, twelve-month-old Giana was drawn like a magnet to the buttons on the computer. Each time she reached for them, her mom gently pushed back her tiny hands and said a firm, "No, Giana." After hearing no multiple times, Giana eventually gave up and found something else to interest her. Given clear expectations, consistent responses, and time, she learned the computer is off-limits. Of course, sometimes a temptation is so strong (like the shiny buttons on an expensive stereo or the pretty flowers on Grandma's valuable tea set) that the easiest solution is to remove the temptation until the child is older and can comprehend and respect the expectation with self-discipline.

Providing young children with clear expectations about responsibilities fosters their ability to experience success and a feeling of accomplishment. Take, for example, the child who knows his teacher expects him to put all the blocks away on the shelf at the conclusion of play. When he completes the expected task successfully, he feels a sense of accomplishment and pride. At that point, the child benefits from hearing an acknowledgment of his accomplishment. This helps build self-esteem and leads him to value his work, further fueling his sense of responsibility and accomplishment. Clear expectations help children discover their abilities and expand their skills.

All children at some point test limits. It is a natural part of growing up and forging one's identity. Testing limits is a child's way of exploring if adults mean what they say or if the boundaries are real. If they are not real, children naturally want to discover where the real boundaries are. When adults do not respond consistently to limit testing, children get confused and feel the need to continue testing. Self-discipline develops when children feel the temptation or desire to defy the expectations but decide to control their wants.

Scaffolding

In the construction industry, *scaffolding* refers to a temporary structure created to support people in building a permanent structure. The term has a parallel meaning in the field of education, where it refers to supporting children with temporary assistance so they can build on or develop their current abilities to a higher and ultimately independent level. Scaffolding can be a very helpful strategy for supporting character development. Behaviors such as showing respect, caring for others, or taking responsibility can be abstract and difficult for very young children to grasp. But we can intentionally scaffold their learning experiences to support specific skill development in these areas.

One example of scaffolding relates to teaching manners, a concept obviously too advanced for babies. Yet we can teach babies, starting between nine and twelve months of age, how to make a sign for "please," usually a circular hand motion over the chest. Adults can consistently demonstrate the sign in appropriate situations as they simultaneously say the word "please." Preverbal babies can easily learn to make this sign. This doesn't mean they have internalized this particular show of manners, but making the sign in appropriate moments is the precursor, or the first step. This is a scaffolding approach to teaching manners. Scaffolding encourages children to move progressively from one level of skill to a more complex level. It's the art of breaking learning into "bite-size" pieces that children can master. Building character is done "one bite at a time" when you intentionally plan to help children build on their skills.

Scaffolding is an approach inherently tailored to each child's individual strengths and abilities. It starts by recognizing what skills children have already mastered and supporting them in the next step of development. Faced with the daunting task of cleaning up blocks after building, a caregiver can support a two-year-old by having the child pick up the larger blocks while the caregiver picks up the smaller ones. This helps them complete the task and feel a sense of accomplishment, thus promoting responsibility and self-discipline.

Practicing Behaviors

Children learn new skills and behaviors by practicing them. The behaviors associated with positive character are no different. Practicing in a nonthreatening environment while receiving feedback and encouragement from a trusted caregiver fosters learning and helps the child embrace the behaviors. Parents, caregivers, and teachers should make it a goal to intentionally provide and support opportunities for children to practice skills and behaviors associated with positive character traits.

In the previous section, we described teaching sign language to babies as a way of scaffolding their development of manners. Signing is also an excellent example of an activity that typically requires a lot of practice. Teaching even very simple signs to a baby may take several months of parent or caregiver modeling before she will attempt it herself. Once an infant makes the sign, she must be encouraged to practice frequently so that the sign becomes part of her regular vocabulary.

Pets can provide wonderful opportunities for children to practice skills demonstrating caring and responsibility. In preparation for acquiring a new pet in the home or classroom, an adult could ask young children to practice certain basic actions, such as filling a water bowl. Explain and demonstrate the action using clear language and describe how it relates to care of the pet. Pet care jobs for toddlers may be as simple as checking to see that a dog has a warm blanket at bedtime or tipping a premeasured pinch of food into a fishbowl each morning. As they grow older, children's responsibilities can expand to filling food and water bowls or sweeping up spilled food or fur. Having scheduled, daily opportunities to practice their skills presents wonderful growth opportunities for young children.

In a child care setting, there are endless occasions to engage children in practicing skills associated with good character. Children can be given simple cleanup chores, such as clearing away trash after snack each day. Caregivers should look for opportunities to scaffold learning when children have difficulty. This may be something as simple as helping the child understand what is expected. Sometimes we can physically place our hands over (or under) a child's hands to guide her body in completing a challenging activity. Ideally our role as caregiver is to help children get started and then support them in completing the task independently. Having consistent daily chore assignments means lots of opportunities to practice skills.

4

 Play as a Strategy for
Supporting Good Character

We can't force children to learn, but we can set the stage to promote learning. As stated earlier, play is the single most important avenue for young children's learning because it is enjoyable and fully engages their minds and bodies, fueling independent discovery. The seminal Swiss developmental psychologist Jean Piaget (1932) argued that play provides children with opportunities to practice and construct what they know. Alternatively, Russian psychologist Lev Vygotsky (1986) asserted that play helps children learn and grow through free and fun exploration and discovery in new areas. Meanwhile German educator Friedrich Froebel, best known as the founder of the kindergarten system, believed that play was the most important platform for children and adults to form bonds that are the basis for mutually respectful relationships (Smith 1997). However you view it, playtime presents rich and varied learning opportunities and is a uniquely valuable strategy for supporting character development. By pointing out the inherent value of play, we encourage parents and caregivers to be more intentional about planning and preparing play activities.

When we hear the word *play*, our mind might automatically jump to images of children engaged with one another in classic games such as tag or dress-up. Clearly those active group endeavors represent an extremely valuable form of play. Yet that is just one kind of play. Play encompasses a wide range of activities and levels of sophistication, all with the common denominator of enjoyment. The noted sociologist Mildred Parten (1932) defined multiple stages of play, each of which serves a unique purpose in children's development. For example, Parten called the earliest stage of play the solitary stage, in which children primarily entertain themselves and do not interact constructively with peers. This stage is valuable in promoting self-awareness, which prepares children for more complex forms of play in the future. At this stage, adults may engage children in simple activities that allow them the valuable experience of focused attention and care.

Parten's next stage is called the onlooker stage, in which children may observe others, intently watching or asking questions, but still refrain from active engagement and exchange with peers. As an onlooker, the child may examine and evaluate situations, which is practicing important problem-solving skills. Next comes parallel play, typical of toddlers. At this stage, toddlers play side by side, perhaps even doing the same activities, but with limited interaction. Parallel play supports the development of concentration. In the next stage, associative play, yet more complex, children may interact to some degree and perhaps share materials, but they lack a common goal. Finally, having progressed and matured through the previous stages, children begin engaging in cooperative play involving true engagement and interaction with peers (Parten 1932).

Within each of these stages, play promotes the development of some specific behaviors that support character development; among them are sensory exploration, object permanence, problem solving, representational thinking, understanding of cause and effect, and relational skills.

Sensory Exploration

Think of play as exploration for young children that can consist of just about any activity that stimulates the senses and/or the motor skills. Piaget called the first stage of child development the sensorimotor stage, emphasizing the importance of the senses and motor skills as the avenues for learning (Wadsworth 1996). Infants use their senses and basic motor skills to begin to construct their knowledge about the world. Parents and caregivers of young children are very familiar with seeing any object within reach go straight into their mouths. Infants put objects in their mouths to explore them with their senses (touch, taste, even smell). Sensory exploration and experiences also help them begin to form impressions of various character traits. For example, a baby will recognize the gentle touches or certain smell of his mother, and those sensations inform his impressions of caring. A toddler will learn to listen for his dog to bark a welcome when he arrives home, and the sound will inform his impressions of loyalty.

Object Permanence

In their first year, children are rapidly learning that objects and people exist even when they are not immediately seen, heard, or felt. Piaget labeled this development *object permanence* and argued that it was a key stepping-stone in cognitive growth and in understanding that others' perspectives differ from one's own, which in turn is central to good character. Activities that promote and build on the sense of object permanence can be a source of significant fascination, enjoyment, and stimulation for young children. For example, the classic game of peekaboo is simple and fun for all involved, especially when the adult gets treated with a child's giggles each time the adult reappears from behind her hands or a cloth. At the same time, the game reinforces children's sense of object permanence and thus builds the capacity to understand and trust that when significant adults leave, they will later return. Object permanence is also the precursor to recognizing that symbols can represent objects; for example, a photograph can represent a loved one, or a set of squiggles on paper can represent meaningful words. Games and play that promote object permanence also help young children practice memory skills and problem solving (Wadsworth 1996).

Problem Solving

Children engage in problem solving whenever they collect information and make decisions based on that information. Most young children are naturally drawn to problem-solving activities and play. Such activities help children develop thinking skills, exercise creativity, gain confidence, and develop responsibility and self-discipline as they pursue goals, encounter new information or obstacles, and have to rethink decisions. We can encourage children to become problem solvers by allowing them to explore, experiment, discover, and work through solutions on their own, allowing them freedom to make mistakes and learn.

Even infants can engage in basic but important problem solving when they figure out how to grasp or move toward a desired toy, or how to move an object to trigger a reaction. A shape sorter is a classic problem-solving toy, beloved by infants. By the time children are toddlers, problem-solving challenges and play can become much more complex. Toddlers love to figure out strategies or solutions to achieve a more complex goal. For example, they might stand on a toy in order to reach another object that is otherwise out of reach. Seemingly simple forms of play are often rich with problem-solving opportunities for children.

Representational Thinking

Representational thinking is the ability to use an object to represent another object, such as when a child uses a cardboard box to represent a car. It is an important milestone in children's cognitive development and is a precursor to using symbols to represent objects and ideas—including speech, reading, and writing. By the time children are into their first year, they are typically adept at representational thinking, and it has become a key tool for play, especially dramatic play. Using representational thinking, young children can create and act out all kinds of scenarios and dynamics, cultivating and experimenting with character traits as they play.

One of the first landmarks in the development of representational thinking is when children can recognize themselves in the mirror, usually by about fifteen months of age. Another important accomplishment is recognizing a friend or family member in a photograph. As children become more skilled with language and expand their vocabularies and their imaginations, the possibilities for play with representational thinking are endless, and its potential to support character development is enormous.

Understanding Cause and Effect

Children love to experience the feeling of control and power that comes from causing something to happen. Experimenting with cause and effect is a wonderful form of play, starting in simple ways during the first year of life. Cause-and-effect play is also an important vehicle for character development. Having a clear understanding of how one's words and actions impact others is central to embracing the qualities of good character.

Babies love simple cause-and-effect toys, such as a jack-in-the-box and musical toys with buttons or other simple mechanisms that trigger songs. As they mature and their understanding of cause and effect becomes more sophisticated, children enjoy creating scenarios explicitly to cause an effect, such as the classic block tower built for the sole purpose of ultimately knocking it down and watching the big crash. Understanding and predicting effects through play become an important tool for understanding and predicting why things happen in the world, including in social relationships. Predicting results is essential for influencing or altering outcomes. For example, a child may start to run indoors, then switch to a walk because he knows he may be reprimanded or could get hurt. The child makes a decision to alter his behavior based on a prediction. Altering behavior requires self-discipline and supports the development of other positive character traits.

Relational Skills

Children's play can also provide rich and diverse opportunities for practicing relational skills. This is one of the most important ways play can support the development of positive character traits. In play, children can try on different roles and traits without worry, fear, or serious consequence. They can experiment with seeing others' perspectives and exploring the effects of relational decisions, all extremely valuable preparation for real social situations. Children experience the deepest relational value of play once they are able to engage fully and interactively with peers. Parten (1932) called this the cooperative stage of play, and it requires a certain level of language mastery and self- and other-awareness.

Cooperative play requires relatively sophisticated communication. For example, when two or more children work together to build an elaborate block structure and then pretend their structure is a busy bridge for cars and trucks going to work, they have no doubt communicated extensively throughout the process to decide on the shape and form of their structure and its ultimate purpose.

Valuable Areas of Play for Character Development

All play has the potential to support children's learning and character development. That said, it can be helpful to think about and plan for types of play that are particularly valuable, including music, movement, art, blocks, nature and science, puzzles and manipulatives, and dramatic play. Each of these play categories provides benefits for overall child development and offers distinct opportunities for building character.

Music

Anyone who has walked the floors or rocked a baby at bedtime knows that music is a powerful way to soothe and calm children. Music can also do so much more. Musical activities are fun and rich with potential to foster character development, as well as learning of all kinds. A study involving one-year-olds found that interactive music classes with parents led to increased smiles and earlier communication skills (Gerry, Unrau, and Trainor 2012).

Many of us learned the ABCs first by singing them at a very young age. The rhythmic, repetitive nature of music promotes memorization, which is helpful for learning language associated with positive character. For example, a song that explicitly portrays positive communication is the classic "Where Is Thumbkin?" which includes the repeated, respectful greeting and response "How are you today, sir? Very well, I thank you." After singing the song, we can encourage children to practice using the words of greeting and response in play.

Playing with toy instruments can empower little ones, helping them experience a sense of control and accomplishment as they make things happen by their actions. This is the foundation for understanding cause and effect. While any noisemaking can foster these lessons, musical instruments provide a particularly wonderful vehicle in that their sounds can be pleasing and stimulate the brain to listen and hear interesting and complex musical patterns.

Group music time can also present opportunities for building relationships and community. When singing together, groups have common breathing patterns, a process that helps us connect with others and feel a sense of belonging. Music can calm a group of young children who are overly stimulated or excited. When singing with a group, a child who is hesitant to sing alone may feel more capable and join singing, relying on others to carry the responsibility of remembering all the words. Group singing can also lead to opportunities for young children to share their music with others in pleasing social environments. We will see eyes light up when we ask a group of toddlers or twos to sing a song for a classroom guest or while visiting with a senior adult.

Movement

Movement is easily and naturally integrated into music experiences and is also highly beneficial for learning and development. Dancing or following the steps of a song can help build physical strength and coordination, important building blocks for physical fitness. Musical movement helps toddlers and twos to develop crucial body awareness in relation to others and the space around them, part of being self-aware. Learning to move in creative ways helps a young child understand their physical abilities and builds confidence in their abilities to accomplish new tasks.

Movement can also be included in young children's play by creating games and activities that involve gross-motor skills, such as jumping, hopping, balancing, and moving in unique ways. Babies enjoy kicking their feet, rolling on a firm surface, crawling, and cruising by holding on to furniture. Toddlers enjoy climbing, crawling, and slithering their way through an obstacle course. Ask a two-year-old to come to you without using her feet, and see how creative she can be. Movement is also simply an outlet for children's energy, helping them understand their abilities and limits, use self-discipline to control their movements, and respect the space of others.

Art

Art activities open the door for children to experiment and express their creativity. It is a highly affirming form of play, since there is no right or wrong way to express yourself artistically. Even babies can be involved in very simple art activities. For example, place two or three different colors of tempera paint inside a gallon ziplock bag, and tightly seal it with clear packing tape. Tape the bag on the floor, and let babies move the paint around inside the bag while getting their tummy time. They enjoy seeing the results of their actions as colors mix and designs shift. The only goal is the enjoyment and curiosity in doing the activity, not creating a finished product.

Through art, children can have endless opportunities for self-expression and experimentation with cause and effect. For toddlers and twos, a blank sheet of paper and a bunch of crayons or markers can be the platform for expressing just about any idea or emotion. Art can also help children process difficult emotions, which can otherwise be extremely challenging given limited verbal skills and life experiences. For example, a two-year-old drew images of a fire destroying his home. Unable to verbally process his emotional trauma, he was able to release it through art and then receive the supportive empathy of a caregiver. Children often have difficulty understanding their emotions and need help with language to describe their feelings. Before they can understand and respect the feelings of others, they must be able to identify their own emotions.

Completing an art activity gives children the satisfaction of finishing a job and doing quality work. When we talk about responsibility, it involves setting goals and completing tasks. Sometimes children are distracted easily and are apt to wander off before they can fully experience an activity. Art allows them to move at their own pace, completing a task in their own timing. Art activities often include problem solving, sharing or caring for materials, and experiences that support the development of positive character.

Blocks

Blocks are classic, simple, yet ideal toys that offer countless learning and developmental benefits for young children, including stimulating creativity, challenging motor skills, and promoting understanding of basic math and science concepts, such as measurement, counting, weight, and balance. One study conducted with eighteen- to thirty-month-old children found that playing with blocks was connected to increases in language development, among other things (Christakis, Zimmerman, and Garrison 2007).

Even very young babies can play with soft or textured blocks that are light-weight and easy to grasp. Offer an infant a small block to hold, and she will grasp it and use her sensory skills to understand its qualities. As infants get older, they enjoy biting blocks, dropping blocks, and stacking blocks, all activities that help them understand the world and how they interact with it. Blocks develop the skill of self-discipline when a child uses self-control and problem solving to stack blocks with a steady hand.

As they approach two years of age and beyond, pairs or groups of children commonly work together at block play, creating structures or entire worlds and talking among themselves about the design or best strategies for achieving goals. Beyond the benefits already mentioned, block play as a communal activity can uniquely support positive character behaviors, such as respectful communication, cooperation, and self-control.

Block play offers valuable opportunities for adults to scaffold children's learning. A caregiver might ask a toddler, "Can you balance this block on top of that one?" This direction sets an obtainable goal and allows the adult to challenge the child to take a step he might not have otherwise taken, thereby stretching his ability. When children succeed in building a special, tall, or intricate structure, caregivers can encourage the activity further by asking the child to describe the function of the building or the uses of specific designs. These questions help the child use language to elaborate on his activity in conversation. They can experience the surge of self-esteem that comes with accomplishment. When the structure falls, as they inevitably do, caregivers have an opportunity to talk about and model a positive response to disappointment.

Nature and Science

Simple activities involving nature and science are wonderful for promoting exploration and fueling curiosity, caring, and responsibility in very young children. Although nature can be studied or observed through a book or a window, for young children, those are poor substitutes to actually going outside. Young children benefit from playing in and experiencing the outdoors, even when the temperature or weather is not ideal. For example, the best way to learn about snow is to experience it by seeing, touching, tasting, and listening to the crunch of boots walking through it. Experiencing the snow helps a young child understand why birds may need help with food or pets may need to be protected. These obvious caring activities are ways of helping children think about others' needs.

Outdoor play can build respect for nature and promote caring for the environment. Helping a baby feel the rough bark of a tree or the smooth, cool surface of a stone helps them experience nature. Toddlers and twos enjoy activities that allow them to feel the grass under them and experience running with the wind across an open space. When two-year-olds run or roll down a grassy hill, they experience a spatial awareness that helps them understand their movements in relation to the environment. These types of activities provide children with information they need to appreciate their relationship with the environment and develop their respect for it.

Outdoor play is rife with opportunities to learn and practice respect, fair play, and courtesy. When children have to take turns going down a slide, they learn to wait patiently and respect others. They may need help learning to wait, but a caring adult supervising and distracting impatient toddlers and twos before they react to their impulsive desires can assist children in developing the skills they need to cooperate on the playground, treating everyone with respect.

When weather limits outdoor play, caregivers can bring nature inside in the form of objects such as pinecones, leaves, and stones. Interesting and unique items fascinate young children and help them understand and respect the natural world. Raising insects, creating an earthworm jar, and growing plants are wonderful activities that incite curiosity. They open the door for children to discover interesting facts or phenomena. The children's newfound interest in nature and science provides opportunities for caregivers to plan activities that guide them in caring for their environment. Watering a plant or feeding the fish is an easy task for most toddlers and twos.

Puzzles and Manipulatives

Problem-solving materials such as puzzles can support young children's learning and character development. They help children develop small-motor skills, which build self-confidence and fuel further learning. They are also excellent vehicles for challenging children to pursue and accomplish goals. This requires self-discipline and integrity to stay on task even when difficulties are encountered.

You can easily find high-quality puzzles with large, colorful, easy-to-grasp pieces suitable for babies as young as six months. Shape sorters are also classic problem-solving toys for infants. But you don't need to purchase something to help young children engage in problem-solving play. Infants love homemade containers into which they can drop and remove everyday household objects. Even basic daily challenges like using the thumb and forefinger to pick up a piece of cereal and bring it to the mouth can be a great form of problem-solving play that stimulates self-satisfaction and accomplishment.

As children get older, they enjoy more complicated puzzles with smaller, multiple pieces. Taking longer to complete, these challenge children to develop patience and perseverance. Puzzle pieces can be difficult to keep track of. When they are strewn about or multiple puzzles are out at a time, pieces can become lost, damaged, or misplaced with the wrong set, resulting in a situation where the puzzle cannot be completed, no matter how focused the effort. Experiencing this consequence can encourage children to learn to develop their organization skills and self-discipline.

Manipulatives are materials that require young children to use and coordinate the small muscles of the hands. Some examples are interlocking blocks or a basket of small cars that can be used for counting and sorting. Activities involving manipulatives can support toddlers and twos in developing small-motor dexterity and problem solving. When introducing manipulatives, caregivers must be sensitive to the maturity and developmental level of children. Young children should never be given objects so small as to present choking hazards if they do not have the cognitive maturity to refrain from putting them in their mouths. Also, objects that are smaller than their current fine-motor abilities can handle should not be offered. Older twos can typically handle smaller pieces, while fist-size interlocking blocks or tubes work very well for toddlers or infants.

Puzzles and manipulatives present natural opportunities for scaffolding skills by an adult. For example, if a toddler has trouble connecting two interlocking pieces, the adult can use verbal cues, such as "twist that piece just a little and then slide it in place," or even physically guide a child's hands to place pieces if necessary. Adults can also encourage young children to stick with the task to completion, thereby fostering a can-do attitude, which is important in learning to take responsibility.

Dramatic Play

Dramatic play taps children's creativity and imagination, challenges their language and social skills, stretches their ability to use objects to represent other objects, and helps them comprehend and process everyday routines and activities. It is a beloved form of play for many children and can be a wonderful avenue for supporting the development of behaviors associated with good character. Often people think of dramatic play as engaging only for two-year-olds and older, but babies and toddlers can benefit from it as well. Although infants do not literally act in fantasy play, they can enjoy the props that are common to their everyday routines and gradually begin to understand them as symbols.

Easy and natural themes for dramatic play include cooking, shopping, running a restaurant, and caring for babies, but the range and variety of dramatic play are broad. A good dramatic play area includes simple props that may be used in multiple ways, such as scarves, loose-fitting undefined apparel that can serve multiple purposes, dolls, dishes, and interesting (but safe) household objects such as pots and pans. Infants enjoy dramatic play props, such as soft dolls and stuffed animals; real kitchen pieces, for example, wooden spoons and bowls; and sturdily constructed puppets that slip on the hands or feet. Older infants prefer hats, purses, and small bags. Toddlers may want to wear small vests with large buttons, hats, and scarves and push a child-size grocery cart around. Toddlers also like to have small chairs they can push or pick up and move, and cardboard boxes that stack. They enjoy toys with realistic features, such as phones, dishes, and lawn mowers. Twos enjoy many of the same items, but having better representational skills, they can imagine a box is a car or a table. They like having role-playing materials, such as notepads for making grocery lists, cardboard tubes that can become telescopes or telephones, and small blankets to use in a variety of ways, such as for capes, clothing, bed coverings, and tablecloths.

Through dramatic play, children often reenact behaviors associated with positive character without being told or invited to do so. For example, in a pretend restaurant setting, a young "server" explained to a customer that they were out of the daily special, pizza. With expert diplomacy, she went on to suggest that the patron might enjoy ordering the cookies instead, as "they were way better." She then explained that if the customer used the magic word *please*, she would be served faster.

Through dramatic play, young children can also face their fears, for example, the fear of a doctor's office visit. With simple doctor's instrument props and perhaps a white jacket, this type of pretend scenario can help a fearful child become more comfortable with the event. Imaginary play encourages children to learn how to interact with others in socially acceptable ways, making it easier for them to experiment and develop ways of working and cooperating with others. In pretending to care for a doll, young children explore all the ways that a baby needs someone to show caring and respect.

High-Quality Play Environments

A creative, safe, and inviting environment can facilitate rich play experiences and thus support the lessons of good character. Play environments should be aesthetically pleasing, colorful, clean, and uncluttered. They should also be safe, organized, and developmentally appropriate. Young children will engage in play wherever they are, as it's in their nature, but we can enhance the quality of their play by creating high-quality environments.

Young children benefit from having a large area in which to move freely, exercise their gross-motor skills, and engage in a wider variety of activities. If a larger space is not possible, then use the available space creatively. Ideally, activities that require more room can be taken outside. If there is not room inside for a variety of play options, sometimes these options can be provided by developing specific themed boxes that can be brought out for use and then stored for the next time. Dramatic play is more about using nonspecific materials, and with their imaginations children purpose them. Therefore, a block can be a car, a horse, or food for a meal. Pretending is the goal.

The environment should be developmentally appropriate for all children, with properly sized furnishings and toys and materials appropriate for the ages and abilities of the children present. Blocks should be the right size for the children's current age, size, and small-motor abilities. Books should be at the appropriate level as well. Faced with materials that are either too advanced or too simple, or inappropriate facilities, children can become frustrated, bored, and even angry. This does not mean a play environment can be high quality only if it contains expensive materials and furnishings. Appropriate books can be borrowed from the library, and toys can be created with everyday household items, as when children use chairs and blankets used to create a fort. Children's play furniture can be crafted from objects around the home, such as a storage crate for a toddler seat or a cardboard box for a toy stove or pretend bus.

Assess a child's play environment by walking into it and looking at it as though you were a child yourself entering for the first time. Get on your knees to view things from a young child's perspective to see if it's inviting. Organization is essential for a great environment and supports children's character development by helping them visualize order and sequence, important elements in building self-discipline, responsibility, and environmental care. Toddlers will learn to take care of their toys much more readily if you have storage systems that are easy and accessible. Storing materials in a logical manner that fits the purpose and helps define the appropriate use will make cleanup much easier. It also helps with playtime. Children can get frustrated when a basket or toy box contains a mixture of random toys (such as blocks mixed with dress-up clothes), because it's not clear then how to use them. Storing toys in organized, logical, and neat ways can facilitate children learning organizational skills and engaging more deeply in their play.

Books contribute significantly to raising the quality of a play environment. Reading books to children beginning at birth is extremely valuable. It translates into special bonding times between young ones and caregivers early on and develops children's larger vocabularies later. The more time young children spend with books, whether "reading" on their own, simply paging through and looking at pictures, or being read to by an adult, the more comfortable they will become with reading and the greater chance they will discover its joys and benefits for themselves. Maximize the accessibility and enjoyment of books by storing them at the children's level and preparing a reading area with cozy furnishings or pillows that invite settling in and spending time.

Books can also be ideal tools for promoting positive character development. In the following chapters and the bibliography, we have included suggestions for books that specifically highlight positive character traits, along with activities for teaching or supporting those traits.

Presenting the Activities

In the following three chapters, specific interaction activities are presented that encourage children to develop understanding of and value for six character traits: caring, honesty, integrity, respect, responsibility, and self-discipline. For each of the six traits, objectives are listed that are appropriate for infants, toddlers, and twos, with each objective represented by a code. This code will make it easier to focus on specific character traits and objectives when selecting interaction activities. You may already be familiar with many of the activities. Our hope is that by including them in this book, you will appreciate and approach them with more focused intention to make an impact in supporting character development.

Each activity chapter also focuses on a specific age range. Our goal was to make it as easy as possible for you to search for appropriate activities, and yet we acknowledge that many activities can be adapted or utilized for children outside the designated age ranges. Knowledge of your children's abilities will help you in selecting or adapting those activities that are most appropriate for your situation. All of the activities included can be adapted with minor changes for either the home or child care setting.

As you read and undertake the suggested interaction activities, be open to developing your own ideas as well. Supporting the character development of young children should be intentional, not left to chance. Yet you can also seize opportunities for teachable moments with your children whenever they arise. Character formation takes place all the time and in every environment with children. They are observing, learning, figuring it out. And don't forget, the most powerful thing parents and caregivers do each day is set an example with their own words and actions. It's up to you to decide which character traits and behaviors you wish to model.

Finally, we want to encourage you again to be patient with this process. Although there is no doubt that character formation is actively taking place in children within the first two years, the process of teaching and supporting this formation is a bit like investing in a bank account with a very low interest rate. You may not see much change in the total from one statement to the next. Yet over time the account builds, and the interest accumulates. Don't engage in character development activities with the hopes of seeing an immediate return but rather with the goal of investing in children's future.

Character Traits and Objectives

TRAIT	OBJECTIVES
Caring	• Children care for and understand themselves. (C-1) • Children care for others and show empathy and kindness. (C-2) • Children care for the environment. (C-3)
Honesty	• Children are trustworthy and truthful. (H-1) • Children are honest, understanding reality versus pretend. (H-2) • Children use honesty in speech and actions. (H-3)
Integrity	• Children learn the importance of being dependable, reliable, and consistent. (I-1) • Children make wise personal decisions. (I-2) • Children do what they say they will do and follow through on decisions. (I-3) • Children show courage in the face of a challenge, a new experience, or peer pressure. (I-4)
Respect	• Children use appropriate language. (RT-1) • Children are good listeners. (RT-2) • Children use good manners. (RT-3) • Children honor the feelings of others and forgive. (RT-4) • Children treat others fairly, respect rules, and cooperate. (RT-5) • Children learn rules and how to be good citizens. (RT-6)

TRAIT	OBJECTIVES
Responsibility	• Children set goals and accomplish them in a timely manner. (RB-1)
	• Children are conscientious and do their best in their activities. (RB-2)
	• Children are accountable for choices, accepting consequences. (RB-3)
Self-Discipline	• Children use problem-solving methods. (SD-1)
	• Children practice self-control with a positive attitude. (SD-2)
	• Children practice anger management and peacekeeping. (SD-3)

5

Character-Building Activities for Infants and One-Year-Olds

This chapter contains activities appropriate for children ages birth to fifteen months, along with specific character qualities that each activity can support. Some of these activities may already be familiar to you, or they may seem quite simple. And yet you may not have thought about the activity's potential to support a child's character development when done with intentionality. With each activity, the possible character connections and objectives are presented using the codes found at the conclusion of chapter 4. A brief description is also offered of how the activity relates to the specific character qualities and objectives. A list of materials needed is provided.

As you go through the following activities, select those that best coincide with the ages, interests, and developmental abilities of the children in your care. During these activities, you have the potential to influence character development if your interactions with a child are appropriately tailored to his developmental stage, readiness, and state of being at any given time. For example, an infant's receptiveness to being engaged with one of these activities or any other type of interaction depends on his feeling comfortable, calm, awake, and alert. Before a certain age, that can be a rather infrequent convergence of states. You (and baby) will be frustrated if you attempt to do one of these early activities when he is fussy, tired, hungry, sick, or needs a diaper change.

If you've picked up this book, it means that you most likely recognize your potential as a parent or caregiver to influence young children's character development, and for that we congratulate you. Your intentional effort to support young children in developing their good character is a vital investment in their future. We wish you success in your efforts.

Building Trust: Responding to Babies' Cries
AGE RANGE: 0–3 MONTHS
Caring (C-2), Integrity (I-1), Respect (RT-4), Honesty (H-1)

DESCRIPTION: Babies cry to communicate their needs—whether hunger, a wet diaper, exhaustion, pain, a yearning to be held, or simply boredom. Caregivers must sometimes be detectives, tenacious in trying to determine the message being communicated. This is a checklist to help you investigate the causes of baby's distress with sensitivity and care.

- Hunger: Gently stroke or touch the infant's cheek. A hungry baby will turn in the direction of the touch, seeking nourishment, sometimes opening her mouth or sucking. Feed babies when they are hungry. Finish with burping and cuddles.

- Dirty diaper: Okay, we know we don't need to tell you how to check whether this is the source of the distress. But keep in mind that diapers need changing frequently, especially in the first few months, sometimes even just moments after you've finished changing the last one. Use diaper-changing time as an opportunity to talk directly to the baby and soothe him with gentle words, tone, and attention.

- Fatigue: Infants need a lot of sleep, during the day as well as night. As a consequence, they are frequently tired, and this can be a source of significant distress. Determining whether crying is due to exhaustion can be tricky because sometimes babies seem more wired and wide-awake precisely when they are tiredest. Check for signs of tiredness, such as glazed eyes, slight redness of the eyes, and/or frequent blinking. Try walking or rocking gently, playing soft music, or simply putting baby down in a quiet, darkened room to see if sleep comes. Some babies need more help than others to fall asleep. Pacifiers can be calming for many babies during the early months.

- Yearning for touch: Infants love and need to be held. Sometimes fussiness stems from a yearning to be in physical contact with a loving parent or caregiver. Try taking a cuddle break or carrying the baby in a sling or infant-designed backpack that enables close contact. Don't be afraid of spoiling the child. Talk softly to babies as you carry them, using your own calmness to help them regain control and become more peaceful.

- Boredom: Infants sometimes just need a change of view. Simply moving babies to a different location can sometimes stop the crying. Try switching your carrying position so that baby faces forward in your arms rather than backward—it may do the trick.

MATERIALS: none needed

Character connection: When caregivers respond to babies' cries, they model caring for others, respect for the infants' needs, comfort, and integrity by being dependable and reliable. They are also building a rudimentary instinctive base of trust in babies. Attending to infants' needs teaches them that they are important, deserving of respect, and worthy of love. By responding quickly and lovingly, you help babies develop the trusting relationship needed to create a foundation for good character in the future.

Sharing a Smile
AGE RANGE: 0–3 MONTHS
Caring (C-2)

DESCRIPTION: Help infants learn to smile by smiling at them. Hold your face about ten inches from baby's face (about the distance on which her eyes can focus in the first three months) and share your happy, loving expressions. The baby will enjoy watching your expressions and will begin responding to them. When you smile, you will eventually be rewarded with a smile in return.

MATERIALS: none needed

Character connection: Smiling transcends languages and cultures. It translates as an expression of enjoyment and a demonstration of caring feelings for others. Sharing a smile while making eye contact with a baby is a powerful way to demonstrate caring. Babies begin to watch and mimic facial expressions immediately after birth (Meltzoff and Moore 1983). They are drawn to smiling faces and will try to imitate a smile (Witherington et al. 2010). Your loving attention to infants helps to build their foundation of self-confidence and positive self-worth.

Smiling Game
AGE RANGE: 0–3 MONTHS
Caring (C-2)

DESCRIPTION: Sit in a comfortable place with baby in your arms or lap. Stroke the infant's cheek three times, counting aloud and saying, "One, two, three, smile!" as you distinctly smile at her. The baby will enjoy the gentle tickle on her cheek. She will also learn to expect your smile and smile in return. Name your expression by saying, "I smile because I love you." Repeat the activity as often as you like whenever baby seems alert and calm.

MATERIALS: none needed

Character connection: Smiles are universal, and developing a routine connected to smiling is fun. As referenced in the previous activity, infants are capable of smiling, and it is an important means of communication and a way to share our caring with them. Making this a game helps babies anticipate smiles as part of a fun experience.

Rhythmic Soothing
AGE RANGE: 0–6 MONTHS
Caring (C-2)

DESCRIPTION: Hold an infant while sitting in a rocking chair. Sing or chant to the rhythm of the rocking or perhaps using a simple rhythmic tune, such as "London Bridge Is Falling Down." For example, you can chant or sing:

> Johnny likes to rock with me, rock with me, rock with me.
> Johnny likes to rock with me, to help him go to sleep.

MATERIALS: rocking chair

Character connection: Cuddling, rocking, and singing are actions that soothe infants and clearly demonstrate loving and caring. This relaxing activity can help baby to experience the sensation of going from an active or even agitated state to a calm one, further building his impression of caring, as well as starting the foundation for his ability to self-soothe.

One-Sided Conversations
AGE RANGE: 0–6 MONTHS
Respect (RT-1, RT-2)

DESCRIPTION: Make it a habit to talk regularly to infants starting from the day they are born, long before they can verbally respond to you. Here are some ideas to inspire you:

- At morning wake-up, say, "Good morning, sunshine!" looking directly at baby. Describe what you see, such as, "You look like you are ready to get up." Or ask, "Did you sleep well?"

- When preparing for a feeding, say, "I bet you are very hungry. Are you going to be like the very hungry caterpillar [a reference to *The Very Hungry Caterpillar* (Carle 1987)]? He ate everything in sight." Talk softly with your baby during the feeding.

- When preparing for a bath, say, "I am getting all of your bath time things out. Here is the soap, here is the washcloth, here is the tub,

and here is a towel. Let's get some warm water for your tub." Describe your actions as you bathe and dry off baby.

- When you're snuggling baby before bed, draw attention to a favorite stuffed animal: "Oh look! Here is the teddy bear. Teddy has brown eyes, just like you. Feel how soft Teddy's fur is. That's a soft bear!" Gently touch Teddy's fur to baby's skin, and cuddle with baby and the bear.

Look for cues from infants to inspire your conversations. When you see a smile, talk to the baby about possible reasons for that smile. If baby gets his body into an awkward position, use that as a conversation starter while you help him adjust.

When infants begin to make sounds, talk to them by answering and responding to their sounds. When baby says, "Ooohh aaahhh," you respond, "What did you say, Lily? Oh, yes. We are going to get down on the floor and roll around. Doesn't that sound like fun?" Be sure to use an expressive voice and clear enunciation so infants can hear the variety of sounds you make and see the movement of your lips.

MATERIALS: none needed

 Character connection: It may seem strange at first to talk to a baby who most likely doesn't literally understand and most definitely can't talk back, but it is nonetheless extremely beneficial for the baby. Hearing language helps infants learn it. Studies have shown that exposure to more, and varied, language during the first years can activate key areas of infants' brains responsible for language learning. Your one-sided conversation also promotes the development of listening skills. In addition, by speaking to an infant gently and attentively, you expose him to the tones and sounds of caring and respect.

Look for the Sound
AGE RANGE: 3–5 MONTHS
Respect (RT-2)

DESCRIPTION: When baby is alert and calm, place him in a comfortable spot on the floor and lie nearby. Speak his name softly and wait for him to turn and look for the source of the sound. When the baby looks and finds your face, smile and praise him warmly as a reward for seeking out the source of the sound. Next, shift your position to the other side and repeat, allowing time for the infant to reorient toward your voice. As the child develops visual acuity along with the ability to sit with support, you can call to him from a little farther away. Whenever he looks at you in response to your calling his name, praise and encourage him by making positive statements, such as "Good listening!" "Hello there!" or "Peekaboo!" Continue the activity for as long as the baby seems engaged.

MATERIALS: blanket to place on floor

Character connection: Infants learn by using their senses in combination with their motor skills. Listening to the voice of a familiar caregiver, then turning their heads to look for the source of sounds is an important combination of actions, representing a small step in the path toward the respectful skill of listening to others.

Finger Munchkin
AGE RANGE: 3–6 MONTHS
Caring (C-2)

DESCRIPTION: Infants enjoy gentle yet playful touches. Pretend to munch on baby's fingers and toes while saying, "I'm the finger munchkin. I'm going to munch your fingers. Yum, yum, yum!" Make munching noises while playfully kissing fingers or toes and smiling.

MATERIALS: none needed

Character connection: Touch is one of the earliest forms of communication for babies. Through gentle touches, infants sense love and form their first impressions of caring. Being touched also helps them develop awareness of their own bodies, including both their bodily sensations and their sense of orientation in relation to others and objects around them. This body awareness is fundamental to later lessons and growth in self-care and self-discipline.

Baby Massage
AGE RANGE: 0–6 MONTHS
Caring (C-2), Self-Discipline (SD-2)

DESCRIPTION: Skin is the largest sensory organ, and massage can be a comforting, relaxing, and pleasurable experience for infants. Choose a warm room, and place baby on her back on a blanket. Use lotion or almond oil as a lubricant on your hands to reduce friction, warming it by rubbing it between your hands. Use both hands, and massage in light circular motions on baby's body.

- Start with the feet, massaging and caressing bottoms and tops from toes to heels.

- Move up the ankles, calves, and thighs, using gentle kneading motions.

- Take both hands and massage each finger, the palms, tops of the hand, wrists, and forearms as you progress to the upper arms.

- Using a light clockwise motion, gently stimulate the belly, moving upward to the chest and shoulders, making circles as you go along.

- Caress the neck with an upward motion to the ears, using your fingers to circle the ears both back to front and front to back.

- Make small circular motions at the temples and on the scalp.

- Complete the massage by wrapping baby gently in the blanket.

MATERIALS: blanket and lotion or almond oil

Character Connection: The sense of touch is important in the development of attachment between babies and their caregivers. In this respect, massage is a comforting method for interacting with a baby. It stimulates the baby's body and increases self-awareness. It is relaxing, providing a special experience of calming closeness between baby and parent or caregiver. It helps the baby understand the boundaries between self and caregiver, which provides early practice leading to the abilities of self-calming and self-discipline over time.

Tummy Time
AGE RANGE: 2–6 MONTHS
Self-Discipline (SD-1)

DESCRIPTION: Place baby on his tummy on the floor or on a safe, firm surface. Before infants have the muscle strength to effectively raise their head, they may find this position frustrating and quickly start fussing. Limit tummy time at first to just a few minutes, gradually lengthening the sessions over time as the baby gains muscle strength and experiences less frustration with the position. Place interesting toys nearby, increasing his motivation to raise his head and look toward the object. Make sure that you as the parent or caregiver are supervising the infant while he participates in tummy time.

Infants may enjoy moving their arms and legs in this position, sometimes looking like little airplanes. As they become stronger, they may be able to use their arms for support and scoot or reach for toys. Some babies will use this position later to help them creep or crawl.

MATERIALS: interesting toys to capture infant's attention

Character connection: Today's babies typically spend far more time lying on their backs than on their stomachs as a result of the American Academy of Pediatrics (AAP) recommendation that infants should sleep on their backs to reduce the risk of sudden infant death syndrome (AAP 2011). While it is extremely important to follow the AAP sleep recommendation, it is also necessary to allow infants to spend plenty of supervised time on their stomachs. Tummy time is extremely valuable for babies, helping them to strengthen their necks, arms, and upper body muscles. Believe it or not, this can be hard work for infants and perhaps their first real experience of working toward a goal.

Roll Over, Baby!
AGE RANGE: 3–5 MONTHS
Self-Discipline (SD-1)

DESCRIPTION: Place the infant on her back on the floor or other firm surface. Use an interesting toy to attract the baby's attention, and move the toy slowly to her side, placing it just out of reach. Offer words of encouragement when baby follows the toy visually and turns to the side. Say, "You can do it, Jaime," as she arches her back and turns to reach for the toy. Allow time for the baby to work at the task, but if not accomplished, provide assistance by gently helping her to roll over and reach the toy. Try the activity again later, moving the toy to the infant's other side and using other toys.

MATERIALS: interesting toys to capture infant's attention

👥 Character connection: Young infants are constantly striving to grow and stretch their abilities beyond what they currently possess. They may not form goals or think through problem-solving strategies in the way we adults do, but they clearly work to achieve milestones. For example, a baby must work, practice, and strengthen her muscles significantly to achieve the feat of lifting her head off the floor to look around while lying on her tummy. Although babies naturally follow a developmental progression, we can help them in small but significant ways to work toward their accomplishments and milestones. Striving to achieve even very basic milestones is the first stepping-stone in development of self-discipline.

Exploring the World
AGE RANGE: 3–6 MONTHS
Self-Discipline (SD-2)

DESCRIPTION: Provide opportunities for infants to touch and explore different textures. Use carpet tape to connect sample carpet squares, each with a different soft texture. Lay the baby directly on the "rug" so as to experience and explore the textures. Help him move around and experience the variety of textures.

Alternatively, take an infant on a "texture walk" outdoors. Make a point to let him feel (perhaps by physically moving his hand yourself) the textures in nature, such as the rough bark of a tree trunk, a smooth stone, a soft, fluffy dandelion, or a bumpy pinecone.

MATERIALS: carpet samples and carpet tape

👥 Character connection: Babies experience and develop their sensory awareness when they explore textures. Such exploration can also begin laying the foundation for self-awareness, the recognition of self as separate from others, with unique personal interests, likes, dislikes, and perspectives. Self-awareness is a key building block for self-discipline.

Baby Sit-Ups
AGE RANGE: 4–6 MONTHS
Self-Discipline (SD-1)

DESCRIPTION: While an infant is lying on her back on a soft surface, gently grasp her hands. If she is ready, she will let you know by pulling on your hands and trying to sit up. Encourage this movement by gently assisting her to a sitting position, supporting her for a few moments, then gently lowering her again. Do this slowly, and watch her use her neck, shoulders, arms, and abdominal muscles as she orients her head toward you. This is a tough exercise, and it takes lots of concentration; don't allow baby to overdo it. Repeating once or twice each day will build an infant's core muscle strength and help develop the skills needed for sitting. While strenuous, this activity is fun and interesting because of the motion and change in viewpoint from lying down to sitting.

Sing or talk to the baby as you support her movement. Rhythmic sounds combined with the movements can make this activity even more enjoyable for infants. You might say, "Uuuup comes baby!" using a voice going from low to high, as you help her reach a sitting position, and "Dooown goes baby!" with voice going from high to low, as you gently help her down to her back. Finish the activity with a warm, encouraging statement, such as "What a strong baby!" or "Wow, that was fun!"

MATERIALS: soft surface

Character connection: A baby has very weak neck, shoulder, and abdominal muscles at birth. Caregivers can help strengthen those muscles while also building a trust connection. The rhythmic movements and accompanying sounds in this activity provide a rich sensori-motor experience while helping infants do the essential work of strengthening their muscles.

Puppet Faces
AGE RANGE: 3–6 MONTHS
Caring (C-1)

DESCRIPTION: Make simple puppets out of baby mittens. The basic cotton mittens designed to protect babies from scratching themselves are ideal for this activity. Draw or embroider very simple smiley faces with only eyes and a smiling mouth on each mitten. Make sure to use black or dark facial features on white mittens so as to create the most eye-catching contrast. This is important for young babies, who have limited visual acuity. Place the mittens on the infant's hands with the face toward the baby, and move his hand as necessary to help draw his attention to the puppet. Speak to the puppet with an animated tone. For example, you could say, "My, don't you have on a happy face today." Eventually the baby will locate the puppet with his eyes and track it while he moves his hands.

A variation on this activity is to decorate baby socks or booties with bright colors and/or jingle bells. Infants will be drawn to look at and reach for their feet. You can also purchase these kinds of entertaining hand and foot "puppets" if you do not want to make your own.

MATERIALS: baby mittens or booties, fabric markers or embroidery supplies

Character connection: Infants are drawn to look at faces and face-like patterns; after all, they represent the people who care for them. Their attraction to faces undoubtedly helps build their foundation of social skills, as they gradually begin to gain information, such as reading emotional cues from facial expressions and distinguishing the identities of their significant people. This simple activity helps encourage infants' interest in faces, thus promoting their social development.

Two-Color Art
AGE RANGE: 3–9 MONTHS
Self-Discipline (SD-1, SD-2)

DESCRIPTION: Place a four-by-four-inch art canvas in a small ziplock bag. Drop two different colors of tempera paint on top of the canvas, and zip the bag closed, sealing it with heavy tape. Give the bag to the infant to handle, squeeze, mouth, and manipulate. When baby is tired of the activity, take the bag and remove the canvas to dry.

MATERIALS: clear packing tape, ziplock bag, small canvas, tempera paint

Character connection: Infants enjoy touching, holding, and manipulating objects. Through such activities, they are actively exploring and learning about their world. Babies also like to make things happen. This activity enables infants to use their hands, and possibly their mouths, to experiment with colors and see results on their canvases.

Baby's Own Mobile
AGE RANGE: 3–15+ MONTHS
Caring (C-2, C-3)

DESCRIPTION: Make a personalized mobile for infants using laminated pictures of family members, pets, or special people. Suspend from the ceiling a short stick, or a set of two sticks secured together in an X, or a clothes hanger, or even a small umbrella (handle pointed up). Attach thin wires or sections of fishing line with paper clips at the ends, to which you can then fasten the laminated photos. Hang the mobile near the infant's changing table or play area, so that the photographs can be viewed easily and become a focal point. Make sure to hang it high enough to be out of reach of tiny hands but close enough for the infant to focus on the pictures. Be intentional about commenting regularly on the people depicted and their love and care for baby.

MATERIALS: hanging structure (umbrella, sticks, or hanger), fishing line or wire, paper clips, laminating film, and photographs

Character connection: As infants gain the ability to focus their eyes, they begin taking in more information, learning about the world and forming impressions from what they see. Even very young babies can visually identify caregivers and other familiar faces and sights. Although photographs are a relatively abstract concept that they will not yet fully grasp, they will enjoy looking at colorful, smiling faces. A personalized mobile can serve as an excellent spark for talking to babies, gently and consistently, about all the people who love and care for them.

Baby Compliments

AGE RANGE: 4–15 MONTHS

Caring (C-2), Respect (RT-1, RT-4), Self-Discipline (SD-2)

DESCRIPTION: Make a point of complimenting infants throughout the day, commenting on their actions and behaviors, using supportive, positive observations. Your compliments offer them the chance to hear a broader array of vocabulary as well as loving and supportive words and tone from their caregiver. Following are some examples of what you can say:

- "Maddie, you waited a whole five minutes for your bottle without crying. You're learning how to soothe yourself."

- "Thomas, look at you playing with your rattle. You're entertaining yourself so well."

- "What a nice kiss. Thank you!"

- "Amelia, great job being so patient while I change your diaper. Now I know you will feel so much better!"

- "Good work getting your doll out of the block box!"

- "Wow, you handed me your teddy bear. Thank you for sharing!"

MATERIALS: none needed

Character connection: Infants are listening to our language long before they are able to speak. They notice such things as the tone of our voices and our body language. Using positive and respectful tones and language demonstrates respect and care. Sharing a compliment with a baby takes only a moment but can make a significant positive impression, laying the first stones in their foundation of self-worth. In addition, you can specifically compliment them as they begin to exhibit the first budding signs of self-control.

Peekaboo

AGE RANGE: 4–15 MONTHS

Honesty (H-1), Integrity (I-1)

DESCRIPTION: Hide behind a blanket and lower the blanket to reappear for the baby. When you are unseen, the baby thinks you are gone. When you reappear, baby is surprised. This age-old game teaches infants that even when one is out of sight, that person is not gone. It builds trust, because even though people disappear for a short time, they come back. This game can help baby build trust in the caregiver to return after being out of sight for brief times. You can vary

the activity by hiding a favorite toy under the blanket. Remove the blanket, and the toy is still there! As babies develop the ability to grasp and remove the blanket, let them do this part themselves. The appeal of this activity endures well after the first birthday.

MATERIALS: blanket, toy

Character connection: Before a certain age, infants cannot comprehend that people and things exist when they do not see them. The game of peekaboo, which helps to develop the sense of object permanence, is fascinating to babies throughout the trajectory of development. Before acquiring object permanence, they experience the fun and magical surprise of a loved one "coming back" after disappearing. Once acquiring it, they have the amusement of knowing the trick and anticipating what the surprise will be. Playing peekaboo not only is a simple way to have fun with and elicit giggles from babies but also sets the stage for honesty by reinforcing the understanding that caregivers can be trusted to reappear and will be reliable and consistent.

Hide-and-Seek
AGE RANGE: 4–15 MONTHS
Self-Discipline (SD-1)

DESCRIPTION: Hide a favorite toy or puppet in your pocket. Allow infants just a glimpse of the toy. Ask, "Where is the doggy?" Let them look for the toy. After they find the toy, let them work at getting it out of your pocket. Many variations of this activity can be planned using buckets, blankets, or other materials to hide a variety of objects. Using variety will keep the game fun and interesting. For younger infants, do the activity in your lap. As babies are able to sit up, place and hide toys in front of them. When babies are able to pull to standing, the game becomes fun at a table. A walking infant will enjoy looking in several places around the room for a hidden toy.

MATERIALS: small toy, pocket, bucket, blanket

Character connection: This activity helps infants develop problem-solving skills, which in turn contribute to the development of self-discipline.

Sharing Time
AGE RANGE: 6–12 MONTHS
Respect (RT-5), Self-Discipline (SD-1, SD-2)

DESCRIPTION: Offer an infant her favorite toy, then, in a short while, gently ask for your turn to hold it. The infant may hesitantly hold the toy out to you, unsure of your intentions. You may have to ask again gently. When the toy is given, say thank you and praise the infant for sharing. After a few seconds of holding the toy, give it back to show that you are also willing to share, saying, "Now it's your turn." Continue to trade the toy, smiling as you do so. This becomes a game of sharing, and the infant has to trust you enough to share the toy. Treat this evidence of trust on the baby's part with respect.

MATERIALS: favorite toy

Character connection: Sharing, taking turns, and showing generosity are ways people demonstrate respect and caring. Infants learn about sharing from observing adults. In this activity, babies will follow the example of their significant adults and experiment with sharing and taking turns. This exercise also offers a basic lesson in self-control by requiring infants to wait for their turn to hold the toy.

Kitchen Drums
AGE RANGE: 4–15 MONTHS
Self-Discipline (SD-1)

DESCRIPTION: Create opportunities for infants to explore and enjoy a variety of sounds. Give them a wooden spoon and a metal mixing bowl, and encourage them to hit the bowl to make sound. Offer alternative implements and objects for experimentation, such as a metal spoon and a plastic bowl or a wooden spoon with a cloth wrapped around the end. Infants will no doubt enjoy hearing the different sounds they can create with the different implements, the different "drums," and different ways to hit the bowls. They will also enjoy having others join in with their own implements and drums—creating an orchestra!

MATERIALS: wooden and metal spoons, bowls and pans

Character connection: Musical activities provide a fun way for infants to experiment and experience a sense of their own power to create something, in this case sound. Babies learn through playful experimentation how to control their actions to change the results. This kind of experimentation is an important stepping-stone to problem solving and the development of self-discipline.

Baby's Personal Album
AGE RANGE: 6–15 MONTHS
Caring (C-1), Respect (RT-1, RT-2)

DESCRIPTION: Fill a small, durable photo album with pictures of baby, family, and friends. Sit in a comfortable place with the infant in your lap and look at the book together. Identify and describe the people pictured. Point to each picture as you describe it. Put the book with other books in your library after the infant has enjoyed it so that it can be used again. As the child becomes familiar with the book, encourage his attempts to name or describe the people pictured. A variation of this activity can be done with even younger infants. Glue pictures to a poster board and laminate. Put the poster board on the floor in front of baby during tummy time. Infants can reach for and pat the pictures.

MATERIALS: photo album or poster board, photos

 Character connection: A book about themselves helps children identify pictures of family and friends who care for them. Knowing they have a circle of caring family and friends helps children feel secure and loved. Through conversation about the people in the pictures, infants hear caring language and can practice their listening and attention skills.

Hand-Washing Song
AGE RANGE: 6–15 MONTHS
Caring (C-1)

DESCRIPTION: Infants do not have the skills to effectively wash their own hands, so adults must help them. Sing this song during hand washing to make it more enjoyable for them and to create a fun routine:

> Wash, wash, wash your hands. Wash your hands with soap.
> Wash, wash, wash your hands. Wash your hands with soap.
> (To the tune of "Row, Row, Row Your Boat," sung twice)

Also describe in simple terms what you are doing as you wash a child's hands. For example, you can say, "First we get our hands wet, then we put the soap on them. Now rub, rub, rub, and get them clean." You can also use this song with toddlers and twos who have more independent hand-washing skills yet would also benefit from the routine of singing as encouragement to take their time with hand washing and wash thoroughly. Although more independent, toddlers still need close supervision during hand washing.

MATERIALS: none needed

 Character connection: Hand washing is an important way in which we take care of ourselves. At this age, infants still need assistance from adults with this process. Babies will enjoy the experience more, and resist less, when their adults sing happily to accompany their actions. Singing during hand washing also encourages adults to take more time with the activity, so as to do it more thoroughly. Focusing attention and spending dedicated time with infants on daily routines such as hand washing demonstrates caring.

Pull the Toy
AGE RANGE: 8–12 MONTHS
Responsibility (R-1), Self-Discipline (SD-1)

DESCRIPTION: Choose two or three favorite toys and tie a string to each (approximately three feet of string for each toy works well). Set the first toy on the floor with the string extended. Seat the infant within arm's reach of the end of the string. Demonstrate for baby how pulling on the string brings the toy. Encourage the infant to pull the string on his own. Once baby succeeds, place another toy nearby with a string (this may be at the same sitting or another time). Show the infant the second toy and string and invite him to pull the string. Infants will enjoy having two toys to pull. Later, when he has succeeded at pulling two toys, place a third toy and encourage him to pull each toy using the strings. Supervise this activity closely because strings can be dangerous choking hazards. Do not leave infants alone with string.

MATERIALS: two or three favorite toys, string

Character connection: Infants enjoy pulling toys on a string. This activity provides them a valuable experience in controlling an effect, making something happen. It also requires problem solving. Babies begin to be able to use objects to help them reach or obtain other objects, an important development in problem solving.

Predicting Results
AGE RANGE: 8–15 MONTHS
Integrity (I-1, I-2)

DESCRIPTION: Lay a cardboard tube on the floor (a wrapping paper tube works especially well for this activity). Place a small ball (small enough to roll through the tube but not small enough to be swallowed) just inside the tube, and ask the infant, "Where will it go?" Children will start by looking in the end of the tube to see where the ball went. Tip the tube slightly so that the ball rolls through and exits out the other end. Repeat the game again, and infants will eventually begin to watch for the ball to emerge from the end of the tube.

MATERIALS: cardboard wrapping paper tube, small ball

Character connection: Infants learn by observing, using their senses, and interacting with their environments. Through their experiences, they develop expectations based on observing predictable events. This helps them begin to grasp the concept of reliability—a key factor in developing integrity.

Filling and Dumping
AGE RANGE: 8-15 MONTHS
Self-Discipline (SD-1)

DESCRIPTION: Provide a container such as an empty oatmeal box or coffee can. Also provide small toys to drop inside. Once the items have been dropped into the container, dump them out onto the floor and start again. Select toys that will interest the children (balls, blocks, rattles, keys). Change the items regularly, so as to add interest and surprise to the activity whenever it is done. Always make sure the small objects are not so small as to present choking hazards.

MATERIALS: empty container, small toys

Character connection: Older babies enjoy filling and dumping, which is essentially a basic exercise in problem solving. They like to get objects into a container then back out again. They also enjoy the dumping because they feel in control. Problem solving is an important part of self-discipline and helps to nurture self-confidence. An infant's ability to accomplish things successfully fosters an "I can do it!" attitude.

How Do You Do?
AGE RANGE: 8-15 MONTHS
Respect (RT-4)

DESCRIPTION: Make a point of holding the infant in your arms when you greet a new person. This provides baby an opportunity to observe the way you show respect when greeting others. Encourage the infant to participate in the greeting process by smiling or waving hello. This activity can also help a baby who is experiencing the normal stage of anxiety or fearfulness of strangers, because it exposes babies to strangers while being held closely in their caregiver's arms without fear of being handed over to the stranger. During a longer visit, you and your adult companion might both sit down. At that point, you can allow the infant to choose whether to stay in the comfort of your lap or leave and explore the nearby surroundings or perhaps approach the stranger. Let that be the baby's choice.

MATERIALS: none needed

Character connection: Role modeling is the most powerful avenue for supporting positive character development. It is easy for caregivers to underestimate our tremendous power as role models for our children. Every interaction you have with other adults in front of young children presents opportunities to demonstrate the traits of positive character. Respectfully and courteously greeting people is a simple, yet important, interaction to model as children begin to face this situation themselves from a very young age. You can also model a respectful and friendly greeting while helping infants feel safe and secure, especially when they are in the midst of the "stranger anxiety" stage, which is common between eight and fifteen months of age.

Say Good-Bye
AGE RANGE: 8–15 MONTHS
Honesty (H-1, H-3), Integrity (I-1)

DESCRIPTION: Good-byes can be painful and difficult times for both children and adults, whether it's leaving children with a babysitter or grandmother, or dropping them off at child care. Usually young children cry because they feel insecure about a parent leaving their sight, unsure that they will return. It is a normal developmental stage, but some children have more trouble with it because of differences in their temperaments. Parents often go to great lengths to avoid pain for their children and the arduousness of the difficult separating moments. In the long run, avoiding the good-bye isn't helpful for the child, and it misses a distinct character-building opportunity.

Children need to trust that adults in their lives are going to return to get them after a short separation. It is never a good idea to leave a child and sneak out. This can lead to the child believing the adult cannot be trusted. The other side of this issue is the adult who lingers too long before separating. Engaging in lengthy conversations before leaving often causes the separation process to be more difficult. Typically, saying good-bye in a clear, positive way, while reminding children that you will return and will miss them during the separation, works. Children may cry and protest, but this is a normal and healthy response and is often short-lived. You may need to post a reminder of the importance of intentional good-byes with young children. This is useful for all good-byes with children.

> Say good-bye to ME,
> Tell ME you'll be back,
> Hug and kiss ME, say you'll miss ME
> Till you do come back!

MATERIALS: none needed

Character connection: Parting moments are difficult for young children but are a time to build trust. When parents or caregivers say they will be back, children learn to trust that they will do what they say they will do.

Cruising Around
AGE RANGE: 10–15 MONTHS
Self-Discipline (SD-1), Responsibility (RB-1)

DESCRIPTION: This activity is designed for infants who are learning to walk and can take a few steps with support. Line up chairs in a row, placing an eye-catching toy or object on every other chair. Help the infant stand at the first chair in the line. Point to the first toy, and encourage baby to move to that chair to get to it. Cheer and clap when she reaches it. As baby moves from one chair to the next, cheer and clap as each toy is reached. Don't be upset if the infant reaches the first toy and loses interest in the game of cruising. You can come back to it again later. As infants gain strength and improve walking skills, they will be able to move farther and stick with the activity longer.

MATERIALS: chairs, favorite toys

⚏ Character connection: Provide infants with challenging activities while offering encouragement and assistance. In doing this, you are essentially helping them set and achieve goals.

Learning to move independently and walk gives babies a sense of empowerment and success. It also takes courage and determination, as well as problem-solving skills. Stay close by as infants cruise. Your physical presence helps them feel supported, and your watchful eyes are essential. Provide verbal encouragement by describing babies' actions and praising their efforts.

Pillow Hill Walk
AGE RANGE: 10–15 MONTHS
Integrity (I-4)

DESCRIPTION: Place a variety of pillows or cushions on the floor, and help infants climb over pillows by holding both of their hands to support them while they walk. As they travel across the cushy surface, they will enjoy the variety of heights and the sensory stimuli of differing resistance provided by the pillows. Use a nursery rhyme, such as the following, to engage the baby in this fun activity.

Mighty Duke of York
Oh, the mighty Duke of York, he had ten
    thousand men;
He marched them up to the top of the hill,
    and he marched them down again.
Oh, when they're up they're up, and when
    they're down they're down,
And when they're only halfway up, they're
    neither up nor down.

Close supervision and assistance are required for this activity at all times.

MATERIALS: variety of pillows or cushions

⚏ Character connection: Exploring new activities while having the security of a loving caregiver makes it easier to face new challenges and helps infants build trust. The sensory experience of body weight on various surfaces also provides infants with valuable practice in walking, building strength and coordination.

Character-Building Activities with Books for Infants

Reading books to young children can be a wonderful avenue for supporting the character values you want them to embrace. There are many books written specifically for teaching character lessons, but there are also countless children's books with generally uplifting, supportive, and inspiring messages or stories. Keep your eyes open for character-teaching opportunities in every book you encounter.

Some parents, caregivers, or teachers may have the impression that reading aloud to little ones is an option only once the children are old enough to focus and comprehend the words and story line. However, you can begin reading aloud to infants within days of their birth. They may not comprehend your words, but during their short windows of calm alertness, they will enjoy and be comforted by being held in your lap and hearing your calm, gentle voice. Reading stimulates infants' interest in language and listening, and the routine becomes an expected part of the day. Select books that emphasize the rhythm and repetition of language to hold an infant's attention. As babies gradually develop the ability to focus their eyes during the first few months, you'll be amazed at their capacity to look intently at the pictures in simple black-and-white board books. Hold the pictures about nine to thirteen inches away from their faces to provide them with the optimum visual focus. Talk about the pictures and enjoy knowing that baby's brain is developing and forming connections with this precious activity.

A few months later, when infants begin to jabber as they look at books, listen carefully and respond. Assume they are commenting on the pictures or the story and affirm their potential thoughts. "Yes, Jack, that doggy does have brown spots. Look how he runs after the boy." Don't worry whether your words make sense or match their thoughts exactly. Your efforts to respond and converse with them affirm their communication attempts and help them develop an impression of conversation as the back-and-forth of sharing and listening.

Read often, but don't worry about reading all the words or finishing the books when children are still quite young. Judge their attention to the book and stick with it only until they show signs of losing interest. Then close the book and move on to another activity until the next opportunity for reading comes along. When infants show a desire and are able to do so, encourage them to hold their own books. Spending time reading to children conveys a sense of caring: "The adult cares enough to spend time with me, speak kindly, and encourage me." Young children generally enjoy hearing the same story repeatedly. Repetition is comforting for children and, as mentioned, encourages the development of trust.

Peekaboo Morning (Rachel Isadora)
AGE RANGE: 6–12 MONTHS
Caring (C-1, C-2, C-3)

CHARACTER-RELATED CONTENT: *Peekaboo Morning* begins as baby wakes up. Peekaboo baby sees Mommy, Daddy, "me," a puppy, a toy train, Grandma, Grandpa, a bunny, a butterfly, and a friend. Rhythmic use of "Peekaboo, I see . . ." is combined with high-contrast, colorful pictures of people, animals, and toys. Ending with the line "I see you!" the sturdy board book is perfect for babies during the second half of the first year. The character trait of caring is illustrated in the engaging portrayal of positive, playful interactions with other family members, toys, and nature.

ACTIVITY: After reading the book, use the illustrations as the basis for this activity. Gather toys that match the illustrations, perhaps a stuffed rabbit, puppy, and a toy train. Also find three small baskets. Invite the infant to look at the three baskets, each with one of the items from the story. Allow the child to choose an item, and then say, "Watch this." Place the basket over the item, saying, "peekaboo," then lift the basket and say, "I see ____," naming the item. Covering items with blankets can be used as an alternative to baskets. Infants will enjoy picking out the toy and seeing it disappear and reappear!

MATERIALS: three toys and three small baskets, three small blankets

When Momma Comes Home Tonight (Eileen Spinelli)
CARING (C-1, C-2), INTEGRITY (I-1)
Age range: 6–15 months

CHARACTER-RELATED CONTENT: This inspiring book is written for working mothers and their babies. Repeated language, rhymes, and beautiful illustrations convey the closeness and variety of activities mother and baby will do together, such as hugs and kisses, feeding, playing games, bathing, and tucking in baby. The words and pictures portray caring relationships and everyday activities. Caring for self and others, loving relationships, and being dependable are clear themes in this simple board book.

ACTIVITY: Expand on the themes in the book by learning nursery rhymes to repeat with baby during busy times of the day. Just like the mom in the book, you can use this simple activity to connect on a one-to-one level anytime and any place. Rhymes such as "Pat-a-Cake" and "Two Little Eyes" are engaging and can save the day when unexpected waits occur and plans change. These special interactions are important to infants and their caregivers.

MATERIALS: none needed

Baby! Talk! (Penny Gentieu)
AGE RANGE: 0–12 MONTHS
Respect (RT-1, RT-4)

CHARACTER-RELATED CONTENT: This board book introduces expressions and words encouraging infants to communicate and try out their verbal skills. Respect for feelings is identified in the different emotions visible on the babies' faces and body language, providing caregivers with opportunities to use appropriate language about the feelings of others.

ACTIVITY: Use this book to try out new sounds and expressions. Be sure the infant sees your mouth as you exaggerate sounds. Imitate the emotions from the book, such as "all gone" or "uh-oh." This book contains pictures of many babies; you can use them to point out parts of the body on the pictures, then play a game of "name that body part." Point to the pictures and say, "nose," and then point to baby's nose. Tickle parts of the body as you name them. "I'll tickle your toes. I'll tickle your knees." Because this book sparks a game, babies will no doubt want to read it frequently.

MATERIALS: none needed

All of Baby, Nose to Toes (Victoria Adler)
AGE RANGE: 6–12 MONTHS
Caring (C-1, C-2)

CHARACTER-RELATED CONTENT: The pictures are playful with just the right amount of rhythmic text to use with infants. Pastel watercolor illustrations depict a young baby and loving family members interacting with the baby in playful ways, talking about all the parts they love. By talking about all the people that love baby, we reinforce the concept of caring for each other. Text can easily be adjusted to meet the attention span of the infant.

ACTIVITY: As you read the words, point out the parts of the body in a playful manner. Memorize the words and use them later when playing with baby on the floor, tickling his belly and toes and hearing him giggle. Playful attention is one way of showing we care about others.

MATERIALS: none needed

My Two Hands, My Two Feet (Rick Walton)
AGE RANGE: 9–15 MONTHS
Caring (C-1)

CHARACTER-RELATED CONTENT: Colorful illustrations make this a fun book to read with infants. This is actually two books in one: the pictures and text for the feet book start on one cover; when you flip the book over, the hands book starts from the other cover. It encompasses a variety of character-related themes that reflect caring activities, such as hand washing, sleeping, and holding hands while crossing the street.

ACTIVITY: Read the "feet" part first, then turn the book over and read the "hands" part while you act out examples of the dialogue. After you have read this book a few times, try memorizing some of the rhymes to use during floor playtime.

MATERIALS: none needed

ABC Look at Me (Roberta Grobel Intrater)
AGE RANGE: 9–15 MONTHS
Respect (RT-4)

CHARACTER-RELATED CONTENT: Durable pages display adorable pictures of infants, making this a fun book to share with babies. Each letter of the alphabet describes a different expression. Photographs for such words as *angry*, *stubborn*, *joyful*, and *grumpy* give a delightful pictorial array of feelings. The message is that feelings are not wrong but an expression of what is happening inside people, and we honor the feelings of others.

ACTIVITY: As you sit with baby and talk about the pictures, try to reproduce the facial expressions and discuss them. Say, "I can look unhappy," or "Yay, I'm excited." Let older infants show you their happy, angry, and grumpy faces.

MATERIALS: none needed

Baby Faces (Margaret Miller)
AGE RANGE: 1–12 MONTHS
Respect (RT-4)

CHARACTER-RELATED CONTENT: This durable board book has fun photographs of infant faces with one-word text naming the emotional expressions seen on each baby's face. Identifying emotions is the first step toward understanding and then respecting them.

ACTIVITY: As you look at the pictures, talk about the expressions on children's faces in the book. What do their expressions say about their feelings? Mimic the expressions seen on the pages. Demonstrate careful touches as you point out eyes, ears, nose, and mouth. What do the eyes, mouth, and face tell us about the way the baby is feeling? Talk about the pictures of infants. How are they different? How are they alike? What is "yucky"? What stinks?

MATERIALS: none needed

Bye-Bye Time (Elizabeth Verdick)
AGE RANGE: 8–15 MONTHS
Caring (C-2), Integrity (I-1, I-4)

CHARACTER-RELATED CONTENT: Drop-off at child care happens daily for many children; this book has illustrations that take the fear out of this transition. Saying good-bye to Mom or Dad is a big deal. This book explains the transition with daily rituals: hugs and kisses, a big wave, a deep breath, and the confidence to seek comfort with the new caregiver or other children. Good-bye is not forever. The author and illustrator provide a fun look at the transitions infants and toddlers face daily, giving them the tools to handle routines with confidence and cooperation, trusting their caregivers and parents.

ACTIVITY: This book is helpful to read with a child who experiences separation anxiety at child care drop-off or any other time when a parent departs. Caregivers should respect a child's feelings if she refuses comforting, yet look for opportunities to hold, cuddle, and reassure her that her parents will return and she is cared for and loved. Share the book and look at the pictures. Talk about what is happening in the story and how she can feel confident that her parents will return.

MATERIALS: none needed

Kisses for Mommy! (Emily Sollinger)
AGE RANGE: 2–8 MONTHS
Caring (C-2)

CHARACTER-RELATED CONTENT: This sturdy board book features bright photographed images of babies and mommies on every page. It includes simple text that is easy to share with a very young infant. The pictures and text tell the story of caring touches.

ACTIVITY: Talk about how Mommy loves baby. Love is evident in a variety of ways. What are the ways this mommy shows her love? Talk about soft touches! Demonstrate soft touches. Practice soft touches on a stuffed animal.

MATERIALS: stuffed animal

Goodnight Moon (Margaret Wise Brown)
AGE RANGE: 6–15 MONTHS
Caring (C-1), Integrity (I-1)

CHARACTER-RELATED CONTENT: This classic book has been a favorite of infants and caregivers for years. The colorful pictures and rhyming words create a soothing cadence as objects, animals, and people come into view and then are told "goodnight." Infants experience caring and consistent visuals and words as the book is read.

ACTIVITY: After you have read the book, extend the ideas by taking baby to the window before bedtime when the moon is clearly visible and shining. Point to the moon, saying, "Goodnight, moon." Identify other objects in the book to say goodnight to, including this in bedtime routines. Another way to expand on the book is to do a simple printing activity with infants. Use a cylinder-shaped wooden block dipped in white paint to print moons on dark paper (black or dark blue). Older infants will enjoy this activity.

MATERIALS: smock, dark paper, cylinder block, and white paint

6

 ## Character-Building Activities for Toddlers

The activities in this chapter are designed to do with children ages twelve to twenty-four months. Many could also be used with older two-year-olds. As in chapters 5 and 7, with each activity the character qualities are listed using the codes found at the end of chapter 4. Also included are brief descriptions of how each activity relates to the character qualities, and objectives and the materials needed, if any.

As you read the activities, select those that best meet the interests and abilities of children in your care, paying attention to their developmental stages and normal developmental progression. Keep in mind that not all children progress at the same rate; each child is an individual with unique needs and abilities.

All of the activities are simple to do either at home or in the child care setting. You may already be doing some of them but may not have considered their potential influence on positive character development. Parents and caregivers are encouraged to be intentional about looking for opportunities to model, introduce, or reinforce positive character qualities in all interactions with young children. Sometimes it can be as simple as taking a few extra minutes to thank a child after an interaction. The smallest gestures can sometimes leave the biggest impressions.

Drop the Cereal

AGE RANGE: 12–15 MONTHS

Self-Discipline (SD-1)

DESCRIPTION: Provide the toddler with an empty, narrow-mouth bottle and a handful of dry cereal. Show him how to drop pieces of cereal into the bottle. Toddlers enjoy this activity, and after all the pieces are put in the bottle, they will turn the bottle upside down, dump them out, and start the game again.

MATERIALS: empty bottle with narrow opening, dry cereal pieces

Character connection: Even very young children can begin learning to solve simple problems. This activity provides basic problem-solving practice.

Soft Touches

AGE RANGE: 12–24 MONTHS

Respect (RT-4), Caring (C-2), Self-Discipline (SD-3)

DESCRIPTION: The purpose of this activity is to help toddlers learn appropriate ways of touching others without hurting. Use an animal puppet to show soft touches. Start with a story to introduce the children to the puppet.

> "This is my friend, Randolph. He likes soft touches on his head. It makes him happy, and he giggles when you give him a pat on the head. Would you like to hear him giggle?" Softly touch Randolph's head and giggle. "When the touching is too rough, Randolph runs away." Touch Randolph's head roughly, and pretend Randolph runs away by hiding the puppet behind your back. Bring Randolph back out and say, "Would you like to pat Randolph's head gently and hear him laugh or giggle?"

Finish up with conversation about the best way to touch someone gently. Practice soft touches with the puppet. Use puppets in dramatic play or with a puppet stage to continue this idea of soft touches. Toddlers can practice soft touches to help learn the distinction between soft and hurting touches.

MATERIALS: soft animal puppet

Character connection: Toddlers are learning relationship skills at the same time they are learning to manage their own bodies and movements and understand their own strength. It can take practice and awareness to learn to touch others in gentle, not rough or impulsive, ways. Modeling gentle touches and practicing on a stuffed animal or puppet is a good way to help toddlers develop the restraint and self-control needed for successful interactions with peers. Gentle touches also demonstrate caring.

Rolling the Ball
AGE RANGE: 12–24 MONTHS
Integrity (I-1), Respect (RT-5)

DESCRIPTION: Sit on the floor facing the child, both of you with legs spread in a V shape and feet touching one another. Roll the ball to the child, and ask her to roll it back to you. Your legs will help keep the ball from escaping easily. You can also expand your circle and include two or three children in this activity at the same time. Toddlers may need encouragement to give up the ball and roll it to you, but they will be excited to see it returned.

MATERIALS: ball

Character connection: Sharing can be challenging for toddlers, who are just starting down the road of learning to see and grasp others' perspectives and feelings. Simple games that require sharing and fair play are helpful exercises. We as caregivers can be powerful role models for sharing and reliability when we consistently share materials and do what we say we will do. Learning to share takes practice. You can help children by modeling the behavior and ensuring every child has a turn in sharing games.

Tickle Time
AGE RANGE: 12–24 MONTHS
Caring (C-2)

DESCRIPTION: Encourage those smiles from toddlers by playfully tickling and engaging in play that makes them laugh. Most children love to be tickled and to receive the undivided attention of a caregiver or parent. Start with a few tickles on the feet or belly, and build until the child is truly giggling. Blow raspberries on his hands or belly. This activity is fun, involves loving touch, and demonstrates caring. Children generally make it known when they have had enough tickling by pushing your hands away, saying, "Stop" or "No." Be aware of this and promptly respect the child's wish to stop. Finish with a gentle hug.

MATERIALS: none needed

Character connection: The bonds of friendship and deep love grow from sharing trust and connections but also from sharing fun, silly times, and laughs together. When adults make time for silly fun and play, they demonstrate an important dimension of caring.

Sharing My Music
AGE RANGE: 12–24 MONTHS
Respect (R-5)

DESCRIPTION: Provide each toddler with a musical instrument. Before you hand out instruments, let the children know they will play that instrument, then swap and play another one. Use recorded music and stop the music when it is time to switch instruments. Make a game of sharing the instruments and start the music again. Fair play means everyone has a chance to use each instrument.

You can make musical instruments from household containers and kitchen equipment. An empty coffee container makes a great drum when you use a wooden spoon as a drumstick. Wooden spoons work well as rhythm sticks. Metal spoons have a nice clinking sound when you strike them together. An empty round salt box can be used as a shaker if you fill it with a small amount of dried rice or pebbles and tape the top down securely.

MATERIALS: various instruments, recorded music, wooden and metal spoons, empty coffee containers, empty salt boxes, rice or pebbles, tape

Character connection: At this age, "Mine!" is a common statement. Toddlers easily feel possessive about objects they enjoy. In this activity, toddlers will share "their" instruments with others if it is presented in a nonthreatening manner and they are confident they will not be left without. Preparing children beforehand to expect the instrument swap makes the transition more acceptable. Learning to treat others fairly, to cooperate with them, and to respect them is difficult for toddlers, but these are skills they can learn with preparation and practice, knowing what is expected.

Voice Character Play
AGE RANGE: 12–24 MONTHS
Respect (RT-2)

DESCRIPTION: Let loose your inner actor and experiment with using different voices when you are trying to get toddlers' attention. It may take a few minutes for young children to notice, but using a different voice can be much more effective than raising your voice. For example, you might use your squeaky mouse voice, "Oh, it's time for us to go to lunch. My nose is twitching because it smells so good." Staying in character, ask children "Do you smell lunch? What do we need to do before we eat?"

Or when it's time to calm down for naps or rest, use a "wise old owl" voice to get children's attention and help shift their energies. You could even use a simple mask to accompany whichever voice you choose. For caregivers, this is an excellent way of capturing toddlers' attention, while at the same time helping them focus on the steps or actions necessary for a transition.

MATERIALS: none needed

Character connection: Before children can be good listeners, you have to get their attention. Caregivers can use vocal creativity and singing to capture the attention of young children. Listening is a significant avenue for learning and a means to indicate respect for others.

Singing Instructions
AGE RANGE: 12–24 MONTHS
Respect (RT-2)

DESCRIPTION: Sometimes children listen more attentively or respond more effectively if you sing instructions. It does not have to be a complicated tune. You can even make up a tune or chant. For example, if you want children to sit, you could sing or chant:

> Sit down, sit down, sit right down.
> Hands in your lap, don't take a nap.
> Sit down, sit down, sit right down.
>
> Or
>
> Stand up, stand up, stand up tall.
> Head held high, back to the wall.
> Stand up, stand up, stand up tall.

Keep singing the chant in a quiet voice as you help toddlers focus on sitting down, standing up, or whatever action you are requesting. Singing instructions helps young children focus on what you are saying—ready to hear important instructions. Attention first, then listening.

MATERIALS: none needed

Character connection: Before children can be good listeners, you have to get their attention. Caregivers can use vocal creativity and singing to capture the attention of young children. Listening is a significant avenue for learning and a means to indicate respect for others.

Signing the Words
AGE RANGE: 12–24 MONTHS
Respect (RT-1)

DESCRIPTION: Toddlers can memorize simple hand signs that go along with songs. Even when they do not sing the words, they can use the signs to communicate the song. Later, you may see a child repeating portions of a favorite song while engaged in play. This is a great way to incorporate sign language instruction. Caregivers do not have to know the sign for every word for this activity to be successful. An excellent simple song for teaching a few basic signs is

"This Is the Way." You can look up designated signs for selected words on the Internet, or you can simply make up your own signs for actions.

> This is the way we wash our hands,
>   wash our hands, wash our hands,
> This is the way we wash our hands,
>   early in the morning.
> This is the way we brush our teeth,
>   brush our teeth, brush our teeth,

This is the way we brush our teeth,
    early in the morning.
(Additional verses may include brush our
    hair, wave good-bye, go to bed.)

MATERIALS: none needed

 Character connection: Language is a primary avenue by which toddlers build relationships and learn to show respect for others while experiencing it themselves. Sign language can be an extremely helpful communication tool for toddlers with limited verbal skills to learn to communicate their needs and wants and begin to show respect for others.

In the Looking Glass
AGE RANGE: 12–24 MONTHS
Caring (C-1)

DESCRIPTION: Encourage toddlers to check the mirror when combing hair, after washing their faces, or after putting on clothes. Make it a game by chanting the following:

    Looking in the mirror
    Who do I see?
    A little (girl/boy) with bright (color) eyes
    Looking at me.

Children may also want to use a mirror to make funny faces. This can be a fun interaction for a child and caregiver as they try different expressions to "outdo" each other with their funny faces.

MATERIALS: mirror

 Character connection: Toddlers are beginning to learn to do many things for themselves as part of their independent self-care routines. Effective grooming is part of taking care of oneself.

Hula-Hoop Play
AGE RANGE: 15–24 MONTHS
Self-Discipline (SD-1), Respect (RT-5)

DESCRIPTION: Give toddlers Hula-Hoops to define "their space." Give instructions having to do with their space, such as, "Stand inside your circle." "Sit outside the circle." "Put your hand in the circle." "Put your foot under the circle." You can adjust the challenges according to the skill level and maturity of the children. The goal is to make sure the children feel successful but, if possible, stretch their learning just a bit. This game is also fun to take outside.

MATERIALS: Hula-Hoops

 Character connection: Toddlers are still refining their motor skills. Developing spatial awareness is an important part of the process that helps them play successfully with others and respect others' spaces. Learning through movement play is one of the easiest ways to help toddlers develop a sense of body awareness in relation to other people and objects.

Dolly's Bath Time
AGE RANGE: 15–24+ MONTHS
Caring (C-1)

DESCRIPTION: Let toddlers replicate their own bathing process with dolls. Provide a small plastic tub of water (one inch of water or less), washable baby dolls, soap, washcloth, towel, and waterproof smocks to keep clothing dry. Place the plastic tub on a low table with a towel under the tub of water to absorb the splashes. Talk with toddlers about how to take a bath, wash with soap, and shampoo hair. Encourage children to describe their actions while they wash the babies, helping toddlers use language to describe the process. "Laura, you're using soap to get your baby clean."

MATERIALS: washable baby doll, small plastic tub, water, washcloth, towel, soap, smock

Character connection: Bathing is important self-care. Even though toddlers are not developmentally ready to manage this activity by themselves, they can practice being in charge of the bathing process.

Mixed-Up Faces
AGE RANGE: 15–24+ MONTHS
Caring (C-2)

DESCRIPTION: Gather a selection of photographs showing the faces of children's individual family members and friends. Cut the photos in half, just under the nose, and laminate the pieces. Make a game of mix-and-match faces. Toddlers will enjoy helping you put the faces together correctly and in weird and funny ways. During the game, talk about how family and friends love and care for us. You might say something like, "Granddaddy likes to hold your hand when you cross the street together."

MATERIALS: large pictures of faces of family and friends, laminating film, scissors

Character connection: Toddlers are just beginning to learn that pictures represent people, and this activity helps them build the understanding and reinforce connections with family members by using photographs in a fun way. Build on the caring connection when you talk about what family and friends do to show they care for us.

Making Choices

AGE RANGE: 15–24+ MONTHS
Integrity (I-2), Responsibility (RB-3)

DESCRIPTION: To help toddlers practice making simple choices, at snacktime offer two different snacks, perhaps raisins and crackers. Allow children to choose one. After they make their choice, talk about it. "Alan, you chose the crackers. Crackers are salty." Encourage children's decision making by recognizing their choices.

MATERIALS: two types of snack

Character connection: Toddlers yearn to be in control of some aspect of their lives, and making simple choices provides a legitimate way to do things "their way." Decision making is an important lifelong skill and challenge. The ability to make good choices that are in the best interests of oneself and others depends on healthy self-confidence and integrity. Decision-making ability and confidence begin with making simple choices in situations where there is no wrong answer or negative consequence. Feeling empowered to make these early decisions lays the groundwork for more consequential decision making later in life.

Helpers Pick Up

AGE RANGE: 15–24+ MONTHS
Integrity (I-2, I-3), Responsibility (RB-2, RB-3)

DESCRIPTION: Turn cleanup time into a fun activity with this simple song that all children can learn and enjoy.

> Do you know what time it is, what time it is, what time it is?
> Do you know what time it is? It's time to clean up.
> (sung to the tune of "The Muffin Man")

Provide several containers, such as small baskets, for collecting toys. Participate alongside toddlers so as to model the expected behavior. Use verbal prompts, such as "Can you pick up the car and put it in the parking spot?" You could even assist children who seem uncertain or lost by using a hand-over-hand approach to guide their actions. This simply involves placing your hands over (or under) the child's hands as needed to demonstrate an action. You might say, "See, this is how we pick up the blocks. You can help me by putting them in the basket."

If children choose to pick up toys, you have an opportunity to praise wise decisions. If children place toys in the wrong basket, you have an opportunity to assist them in finding the right place for that toy. If children choose not to help, accept it and move on—praise when they help. Make the activity fun and they will want to participate.

MATERIALS: small baskets for collecting toys

Character connection: Toddlers enjoy being helpful, and it builds important feelings of self-worth. Helping with very simple chores around the home or child care center is the beginning of embracing responsibility for helping family and friends. Even though tasks take longer when toddlers perform them, it is important to allow them to participate in daily activities and begin to accept responsibility for certain jobs. "Helpers Pick Up" and the following three activities are all great first chores for young children. There are other possibilities as well; think about tasks they can handle that allow them to feel helpful and successful. Assisting with chores is also an important aspect of caring for one another.

Feeding the Monster
AGE RANGE: 12–24+ MONTHS
Responsibility (RB-2), Caring (C-1, C-2, C-3)

DESCRIPTION: Decorate a covered trash can with eyes to make it look like a monster. Decorations can be painted on or glued. After a meal, toddlers will enjoy an activity of feeding the monster trash can their used napkins or food wrappers, complete with monster munching sounds. Encourage them to clean up by throwing away their own waste. Talk to children as they clean up, and help them notice when trash is left behind.

MATERIALS: monster eyes, covered trash can

Character connection: Having a job is fun for toddlers, but a variety of jobs helps them build those feelings of self-worth by providing multiple opportunities for success. Putting trash in the monster trash can encourages them to keep the environment neat and clean, responsible for their own cleanup after eating.

Setting the Table, Part One
AGE RANGE: 18–24 MONTHS
Caring (C-1, C-2, C-3), Responsibility (RB-1, RB-2)

(Note: "Setting the Table, Part Two" is in chapter 7)

DESCRIPTION: Invite toddlers to help get ready for a meal by setting out napkins or place mats around the table. Show them approximately where to place the napkins or place mats, and recognize each step as an accomplishment. Toddlers may not stay focused to complete the job, but don't worry about that. Thank them after any amount of participation.

MATERIALS: napkins or place mats

Character connection: Toddlers enjoy being helpful, but finding jobs where they can be successful is challenging. They will recognize this task as an important responsibility, necessary to the daily routine of mealtime. By assisting with part of the routine, they learn to care for others.

Sorting Socks
AGE RANGE: 18–24+ MONTHS
Responsibility (RB-2)

DESCRIPTION: Sorting socks can be a simple task that facilitates a feeling of accomplishment for toddlers. Place all the socks in a basket, and let toddlers sort them into groups. This might not necessarily be finding two of a kind, though some toddlers may be able to match socks, but can be sorting of big (adults') socks and little (children's) socks. Praise their efforts, and don't worry if they do not stick with the task until it is finished. Any contribution is a step in the right direction.

MATERIALS: clean socks with distinct colors and sizes

Character connection: An important part of helping each other is accepting responsibility for jobs that help the family or group. Sometimes jobs are fun. When a job is a fun part of the day or a learning activity, it becomes an activity that toddlers look forward to doing, anticipating their inclusion in the work while teaching them to develop skills that are helpful.

Spring Cleaning
AGE RANGE: 18–24+ MONTHS
Caring (C-3), Responsibility (RB-1, RB-2)

DESCRIPTION: Have a "spring cleaning" day. Engage toddlers in deeper-than-normal cleaning, including such tasks as wiping down shelves or cubbies, washing windows, or washing waterproof toys in tubs of soapy water and laying them out to dry. Point out dirty spots on toys and furniture, and demonstrate how they can be removed with a damp cloth. Invite children to inspect toys for broken parts or tears by first showing them what a broken toy looks like. Describe your goals: "I want our toys and our room to be clean and safe."

MATERIALS: damp cloths and soapy water

Character connection: Although the children's efforts won't be thorough, and you will still have to undertake (or help to complete) thorough cleaning, this exercise helps children appreciate regular cleaning and inspection as a step in creating a safe and healthy environment. When toddlers see you cleaning, inspecting, and repairing equipment and toys, you model caring for the environment by keeping it safe, neat, clean, attractive, and in good repair. Toddlers love to help and can participate in the process of keeping their rooms neat and safe if they are given clear expectations for the job.

What Do We Bite?
AGE RANGE: 18–24+ MONTHS
Caring (C-1, C-2), Respect (RT-4, RT-5), Self-Discipline (SD-2, SD-3)

DESCRIPTION: Present a set of objects, and invite toddlers to sort them into "bite" and "don't bite" groupings. Items you might include in this game include an apple, teething toy, washcloth, and photographs of friends or other people. Talk with toddlers about why things in the "bite" group are good to bite. Talk about why we do not bite other people. "It hurts!" If biting is the result of a toddler being angry or upset, suggest other options for expressing anger.

This also is a great time to discuss what to do when someone tries to bite you. If children have the language skills, instruct them to use loud words to protect themselves, such as "No!" or "Stop!" Tell children to move quickly from a child who is attempting to bite and to tell an adult.

MATERIALS: apple, teething toy, washcloth, and pictures of friends

👥 **Character connection:** Toddlers are just beginning to learn about respectful interactions with others and appropriate management of feelings. Angry and upset feelings can be especially difficult to handle at this age. Biting is a common and natural urge when toddlers feel extremely upset. This activity can be a tool for helping young children think about right and wrong ways to use teeth. Thinking it through and being told behavioral expectations can help them develop self-control for when conflicts arise.

Snowball Toss
AGE RANGE: 18–24+ MONTHS
Self-Discipline (SD-1, SD-2), Respect (RT-5)

DESCRIPTION: Create an indoor blizzard. Wad up pieces of paper to make snowballs. Have the toddlers wait for your signal to start. Then toss the snowballs at one another. When you are done with the blizzard, recycle the snowballs. Or save them in a box or basket for the next indoor blizzard. You can also make a game of tossing snowballs at an easy target, such as a box or basket.

When you are done with the activity, you can use it as a springboard to discuss what kinds of items can be thrown indoors and which cannot. Select several items and display them for toddlers to examine and sort. Ask, "Which things can you throw inside?" For example, you could present your homemade snowballs and scarves as the throwable items and toy trucks and blocks as the nonthrowable items. Once children have sorted, you could ask them why the nonthrowable items are not used for indoor throwing. The correct answer is, "They are hard and could hurt someone," while the paper snowball and scarf are soft and can be thrown without risk of hurting others.

MATERIALS: paper for making snowballs, two kinds of toys or objects that can be safely thrown indoors and two that should not be thrown, box or basket

Character connection: Toddlers commonly have the urge to throw things as a way of exerting their power, not to mention channeling their energy. Yet most objects are inappropriate for indoor throwing, and thus toddlers may frequently hear the negative message "No throwing." It can be a wonderful, freeing, and empowering experience for them to be invited to throw things indoors to their heart's content. This activity allows them to unleash pent-up energy and to experience a sense of power. At the same time, it can serve as a springboard for discussing reasons for the "no throwing" rule with most indoor objects. This activity can help them develop self-discipline and respect for others and their environment.

Private Speech
AGE RANGE: 18–24+ MONTHS
Respect (RT-1), Self-Discipline (SD-1)

DESCRIPTION: Talk aloud to yourself when you are problem solving so that children can hear your words and thinking. For example, you might say the following:

- [When organizing supplies] "Now where should I put the supplies so that everyone can reach them when they need to? If I put them on this shelf, the children can't reach them because they're too high. This shelf is better. Everyone can reach this one. Yes, I think I'll put them here."

- [When distributing materials] "There are three children here, so I will need to get three pieces of paper for our activity."

- [When cleaning up] "I think I will start by picking up the big blocks. Then I can stack the smaller blocks on top, and they will all fit on the shelf much better."

- [When deciding what outerwear to put on] "I see that it is raining right now. I will wear my raincoat when we go outside so my clothes don't get wet."

- [When deciding what to eat for snack] "I see we have a choice of orange or apple slices. I think I will have apple slices for my snack since I already ate an orange today at breakfast."

MATERIALS: none needed

Character connection: This type of private but verbalized problem solving helps toddlers to understand the process you use to solve problems. It also gives them a language framework for solving their own problems. Young children often chatter away to themselves, and this should not be seen as disruptive behavior but actually helpful for their language acquisition and cognitive development. When you role-model this type of "private speech," you demonstrate that it is a normal and helpful behavior.

Listening Walk
AGE RANGE: 18-24+ MONTHS
Respect (RT-2)

DESCRIPTION: Take toddlers on a listening walk outside. Prepare the children by explaining that they will need to be quiet so they can focus on using their ears to listen. In advance, find simple pictures depicting the sources of sounds you are likely to hear. For example, you might include a garbage truck picking up trash, cars driving by, children playing, crickets chirping, birds singing, and dogs barking. Glue the pictures on index cards, and laminate them for durability. Show children the cards before you begin. During the walk, stop at a convenient spot to display the cards, inviting the children to take turns pointing to pictures representing sounds they heard.

Use simple phrases to talk about listening, such as, "Ears are for listening." Extend this activity by talking about caring for our ears. "Cover your ears when sounds are too loud." Label and demonstrate inside and outside voices. Inside we use a soft voice, while loud voices are for outside play.

MATERIALS: pictures to match to sounds, index cards, laminating film

Character connection: Listening is an essential part of respectful communication. Intentional practice can help us all become better listeners. Sometimes children are so overwhelmed by audio stimuli that they can't hone in on individual sounds. Calling their attention to individual sounds can help them improve their listening skills.

Learning to Follow Rules
AGE RANGE: 18-24+ MONTHS
Caring (C-2), Integrity (I-3), Respect (RT-5)

DESCRIPTION: The key to helping children learn to successfully follow rules is being very clear with them about what the rules are and how you expect them to respond. Rules should be few in number (determined by the age of the child), concise in wording (shorter is better), and positive in their approach.

A simple, easy first rule for toddlers is "be kind." The expectation is "you will treat others gently with respect and help take care of one another." Part of teaching the rule is explaining it to children. If you don't make clear what is expected, the children will have difficulty following the rules. You may have to define the words in language they can understand and be ready to demonstrate what you mean. For example, "I'm going to help Dylan pick up his art project. Then he can join the circle too." Be prepared to guide children to operate within the framework of the rules. You can help toddlers remember the rules by setting them to music. It makes learning easier. Here is an example of a rule song:

Be nice, nice, nice to your friends
Be nice to your friends at school.
Be nice, be nice, be nice, be nice,
Be nice to your friends at school.
(sung to the "Row, Row, Row Your Boat" tune)

MATERIALS: none needed

👥 Character connection: Respecting rules is difficult for toddlers because they are still working on language learning and impulse control. They are beginning to understand what is and is not acceptable. Having rules won't guarantee children will do the right thing, but they are a great way to teach children what the right thing is. Explaining the reasons for certain rules can make children more likely to follow them. Enforcing rules consistently is also important. If you ignore a rule infraction one time but then discipline a child the next time, they become confused and don't know when to trust you. Children respect rules when expectations are clear and rules are consistently enforced.

Following the Schedule
AGE RANGE: 15–24 MONTHS
Integrity (I-1), Responsibility (RB-1), Honesty (H-1, H-3)

DESCRIPTION: Create a picture timeline depicting your daily schedule, and post it on a wall at a child's eye level. Your timeline might include photographs of the child(ren) during daily routines, such as eating meals, napping, playing, brushing teeth, and going to bed. If you are a child care provider, you might depict scheduled events, such as circle time, lunch, centers, rest time, and departure. Toddlers can look at the timeline and understand what to expect and also begin to comprehend the concept of sequencing.

MATERIALS: tagboard, photos, markers, tape

👥 Character connection: Following a schedule helps children anticipate routines and understand your expectations. Knowing what to expect helps toddlers feel safe and capable. Also, when you do what they anticipate in fulfilling your part of the schedule, you are modeling integrity, responsibility, and honesty, helping build their trust in you.

Routines Book
AGE RANGE: 18–24 MONTHS
Integrity (I-1), Responsibility (RB-1), Honesty (H-1, H-3)

DESCRIPTION: For older toddlers, create a personal book about their daily routines. Take pictures of children participating in all the routines that make up the day: getting up in the morning, getting dressed, eating, napping, playing, and listening at story time. Put the pictures in a photo album in sequential order. When a toddler asks what comes next, he can answer his own question by looking for the right pictures. Help him understand by guiding him with words like, "Jay, this is a picture of you eating lunch. We just finished lunch. What does the next picture show you doing?"

MATERIALS: photo album and photos

Character connection: Following a schedule helps children anticipate routines and understand your expectations. Knowing what to expect helps toddlers feel safe and capable. Also, when you do what they anticipate in fulfilling your part of the schedule, you are modeling integrity, responsibility, and honesty, helping build their trust in you.

Cozy Corner
AGE RANGE: 15–24+ MONTHS
Self-Discipline (SD-2, SD-3)

DESCRIPTION: Create a cozy corner retreat for young children. This is not a "time-out" space but rather a safe place for children to go when they need to cope with upset feelings or intense anger. It is a place where they can recover their calm. Make the space inviting by providing soft pillows or a blanket. It can be in a corner, under a bed, or even inside a large appliance box. Invite toddlers to help create this special place and add calming items, such as a favorite stuffed animal or blanket. Introduce them to the concept at a moment when they are not struggling with difficult feelings so you can describe it in positive terms. Develop a verbal signal, such as "Look," or gesture the toddler will recognize when behavior is unacceptable. This may be the time to say, "Do you need to go to your cozy corner?" or if the situation escalates, "It's time to go to your cozy corner." Once in the cozy corner, let the toddler decide when she is ready to leave and interact calmly with people again. Given time and with repetition, toddlers can learn to take themselves to the cozy corner when they need to regroup.

MATERIALS: large box, pillows, blanket, comforting self-soothing items

Character connection: Toddlers are beginning to experience intense feelings they don't understand and may not have good ability to control. These feelings sometimes manifest in pouting, crying, or full-blown tantrums with feet and fists beating the floor. We can help young children deal with out-of-control feelings by responding in a calm manner. The cozy corner is a positive approach and provides strategies for them to practice self-control, helping them manage intense feelings.

Waiting to Eat
AGE RANGE: 18–24+ MONTHS
Self-Discipline (SD-2), Respect (RT-3)

DESCRIPTION: While waiting for mealtime, play a game of keeping hands hidden in one's lap until it is time to eat. By focusing on keeping hands in the lap, children are distracted from their desire to start eating as soon as food appears. The adult starts the game by saying, "Hands are hidden in laps. When I close my eyes, you can start marching your fingers up to your chin, but when I open my eyes, freeze." The adult covers her eyes and, after a few seconds, opens her eyes to see if anyone's hands are moving. "Oops! I see A.J.'s hands moving." Similar to the traditional game Red Light, Green Light, the key is distraction. When a child's hands reach the chin, the adult cheers and says, "Let's start again. Hands in lap." Keep reminders as positive as possible and model what you teach.

MATERIALS: none needed

Character connection: Learning to wait patiently can be difficult for adults and even harder for young children. It takes self-discipline, which toddlers are just beginning to learn. Waiting to eat takes particular self-control because hunger pangs can be uncomfortable. Toddlers learn to demonstrate patience by having opportunities to practice it. Engaging children in conversation will help them practice waiting by distracting them.

Using Nursery Rhymes
AGE RANGE: 18–24+ MONTHS
Respect (RT-2), Self-Discipline (SD-2)

DESCRIPTION: Nursery rhymes are perfect tools for teaching, entertaining, and distracting children during restless times. Nursery rhymes tell stories with vivid images, and they have simple, catchy rhythms with predictable rhyming words at the ends of phrases. Young children often come to know them so well they can easily point out when one is recited incorrectly. Chant a nursery rhyme using a steady rhythm, ending each phrase with an incorrect and even silly word. Pause to allow toddlers to complete the phrase by filling in the correct word. After children fill in the blank, repeat the phrase correctly and move on to the next line. Here is an example:

> Humpty Dumpty sat on a (horse?). No, it was a _____ .
> Humpty Dumpty had a great (jump?) _____ .
> All the king's (bananas?) _____ ,
> And all the king's (monkeys?) _____ ,
> Couldn't put Humpty Dumpty together again.

This activity can be a very helpful and fun distraction when you find yourself having to wait for something for more than a few minutes with children in tow.

MATERIALS: none needed

👥 Character connection: Listening is an important skill for showing respect and care. This activity engages children in listening carefully for mistakes in simple rhymes. Even if a rhyme is not familiar to them, they can often guess the correct word by listening to the rhym-ing patterns. Recognizing rhyming patterns is an important literacy skill. Using this as a fun activity during times of potential restlessness or impatience can help children practice patience and coping skills. Be sure to praise them when they behave well during times of waiting.

Make-Believe Bus
AGE RANGE: 18–24+ MONTHS
Honesty (H-2)

DESCRIPTION: Encourage imaginative play with older toddlers. Place several child-size chairs in a line, creating a "bus." Say, "Let's pretend this bus is going to the store. Does anyone want to go with me?" Be sure you play the part by adding in pretend bus sounds, such as the horn blowing and wheels screeching. After play is over, have fun talking about your pretend trip and say, "We didn't really go to the store, but it was fun to pretend."

MATERIALS: chairs

👥 Character connection: Older toddlers begin to develop the ability to use their imaginations, a step toward understanding the difference between real and pretend. Honesty is grounded in this understanding.

Knuckle-Bump Fireworks
AGE RANGE: 18–24+ MONTHS
Integrity (I-3)

DESCRIPTION: Children need feedback from caregivers about their successes. When they make the right decision, reward them with a knuckle bump ending in fireworks. Do this by making a fist and bumping it with the child's fist. After the bump, bounce the hand back, and spread the fingers using appropriate fireworks sounds to indicate a starburst pattern in the sky. This brief and simple activity yields major dividends in terms of joy and satisfaction for children. You could even add a double knuckle bump for extraspecial times.

MATERIALS: none needed

👥 Character connections: Encouragement helps toddlers learn. Whenever they are successful in a small step toward learning a new skill, reinforce their efforts by recognizing the accomplishment. This encourages them to take another step in the learning process. It affirms and helps them understand when they have made good decisions or choices.

Character-Building Activities with Books for Toddlers

As mentioned in chapter 4, reading to young children can be a wonderful avenue for teaching and supporting character development, either through talking about and observing illustrations or main ideas from the book's content, or by simply experiencing precious, focused time together, and thereby reinforcing and modeling the caring attitudes and respect we want our children to embrace. Young children cherish the time you spend with them. The point of these activities is not primarily to engage toddlers in conversations, as some won't even be speaking more than a few words yet; rather, the point is to simply expose them gently and repetitively to the ideas of caring, respect, self-discipline, and honesty, trusting that they will absorb the messages found in the books and in our interactions and language during reading time.

When reading with toddlers, it is not always important to read every word or turn every page. Reading time should be a joy and not a chore. If a toddler loses interest after the first few pages or is so caught up in what happens on the first page that you can't continue, adjust your reading time to meet the child's needs. When reading, you can create more interest in a story by using various strategies, such as different voices to read parts of the story. Make it about their enjoyment of reading and not about finishing a book.

The following is by no means a comprehensive list of books for sharing character lessons—there are many others—but it is a selected sampling of books found to be valuable, along with ideas for how to use the books to guide children's thoughts and understanding of values.

I Love My Mommy Because . . . (Laurel Porter-Gaylord)
AGE RANGE: 15–24+ MONTHS
Caring (C-2), Integrity (I-1, I-4)

CHARACTER-RELATED CONTENT: Beautiful illustrations and simple text combine in this book to indicate ways animal mothers care for their babies with the same tender love as human mothers. Caring behavior is shown in many ways, such as when the mama cat listens to the baby cat. Mommy feeds and cleans her baby, takes baby for a ride, hugs baby, keeps baby safe and warm, and comes when called, and baby is not afraid of the dark—all because the mother cares and can be relied on to meet her baby's needs. In many cases, a lot of different people care for toddlers, so be sensitive to children who may not have a mother in the home. You can adapt the story for varying families.

ACTIVITY: Make a game of "Who Cares for Me?" After reading the book, ask children questions about their caregivers. Sample questions include the following:

Who gives you a bath?
Who gives you a hug?
Who helps you put on your coat?
Who plays outside with you?
Who watches over you at night?
Who carries you when you're tired?
Who fixes your toy when it breaks?

MATERIALS: none needed

I Love My Daddy Because . . . (Laurel Porter-Gaylord)
AGE RANGE: 15–24+
Caring (C-2), Integrity (I-1, I-4)

CHARACTER-RELATED CONTENT: Similar to *I Love My Mommy Because . . .* , this book illustrates human and animal dads showing tender, loving care for their children by being providers, protectors, and role models. This book provides opportunities to talk about Daddy or other important men in the child's life, such as uncle, grandfather, or special family friend. Be sensitive to children who do not have a father living in the household.

ACTIVITY: Following in the path of the previous game, ask questions in an activity that highlights the caregivers in a child's life. You might ask these questions:

Who helps take care of you?
Who plays with you?
Who keeps you safe and warm?
Who makes you laugh?
Who reaches high things for you?
Who reads to you at bedtime?

Add to the game by providing pictures of caring adults, including the child's caregivers, and let the child pick out the pictures of the caregivers he knows personally.

MATERIALS: pictures

Hug (Jez Alborough)
AGE RANGE: 18–24+ MONTHS
Caring (C-2), Respect (RT-4)

CHARACTER-RELATED CONTENT: This book has colorful illustrations with limited text and depicts hugs shared by a variety of jungle animals. Little Bobo needs a hug, but where is his mother? The caring elephant takes him to find his mother, and when she sees him, she gives him a big hug. Read the book and talk with toddlers about how we show people we care for and respect them. Sometimes families and friends show they love each other by hugging.

ACTIVITY: Play the hugging game. Every time you ring a bell, the children will find someone and ask, "May I hug you?" Some children may not want their space invaded for a hug. Respect a child's preference. Invite those children to give a pat on the back or a handshake instead. Practice keeping the hugs gentle and respectful.

MATERIALS: none needed

Excuse Me! (Karen Katz)
AGE RANGE: 12–24 MONTHS
Respect (RT-3, RT-5)

CHARACTER-RELATED CONTENT: This book teaches the ABCs of polite behavior in a fun way. Toddlers love hearing about other children doing the things they do. It helps them learn respectful, appropriate responses to each situation. The text is simple and easy for a young child to memorize.

ACTIVITY: Learning good manners takes time, but you can make it more fun by combining it with learning sign language. Model the manners you expect at home and away from home by teaching the signs for "thank you" (touch chin with fingertips of flat hand and move the hand outward), "please" (rub chest with flat hand in circular motion), and "more" (touch fingertips together). Practice the words we use to express our manners so as to help toddlers remember them. Make it an activity at a designated meal- or snacktime by asking children to communicate with at least one sign sometime during the meal.

MATERIALS: none needed

Penguin Says "Please" (Michael Dahl)
AGE RANGE: 12–24 MONTHS
Respect (RT-4, RT-3)

CHARACTER-RELATED CONTENT: This sturdy board book for young children has fun illustrations and simple text. A very young penguin demands his way, but his mother guides him to use kind words to ask for what he needs. After a few reminders, he remembers to be courteous, a sign of respect.

ACTIVITY: Make a penguin puppet out of an old black sock. Use white felt pieces hot-glued to the sock for the chest and face, and gold felt for a beak. Use a black marker to draw eyes. Using the sock puppet, act out Penguin's requests: "I'm hungry; give me something to eat." "I'm cold; give me my socks!" His mother reminds him, "First, you must say please." Sometimes toddlers like to use the puppet and say the words. When reading the book, use exaggerated expression to emphasize the word *please*. If you read this book often enough, toddlers will anticipate the words and say them with you.

MATERIALS: small black socks, black marker, gold or yellow and white felt, hot glue gun

No Biting! (Karen Katz)
AGE RANGE: 12–24 MONTHS
Respect (RT-4), Self-Discipline (SD-2)

CHARACTER-RELATED CONTENT: This is a fun book to read to young toddlers. It has simple text and bright, colorful illustrations. The questions it poses help young children understand when it is and is not appropriate to bite, kick, hit, and push—all actions that toddlers sometimes struggle with when they are learning to respect others and develop self-control. Sometimes when toddlers respond in negative ways, it is because they don't see other solutions. Give them options.

ACTIVITY: Make an alligator puppet using a small paper sack. From green construction paper, cut an oval shape to represent the alligator's head, and glue it to the sack. Use white construction paper to create paper teeth. Draw eyes and other features as you choose. After reading the book, bring out your alligator puppet. Using the puppet, pretend to munch on the toddler's arm. "Oh, no! Arms aren't for biting. Let's find an apple." Continue to try different things to bite and decide if they are appropriate for biting or not. For example, you could present a rock, a carrot, a plant, or a cracker.

MATERIALS: small lunch-size paper sack, green and white construction paper, markers or crayons, glue, variety of materials for puppet to bite

Bedtime (Elizabeth Verdick)
AGE RANGE: 12–24 MONTHS
Caring (C-1)

CHARACTER-RELATED CONTENT: This book is helpful for easing toddlers into the get-ready-for-bed routine. With the help of Mom and Dad, a sister and brother enjoy snacks, relaxing baths, teeth brushing, stories, lullabies, back rubs, and hugs. The illustrations and text help children accept bedtime as a positive experience. "And I do my best growing when I'm sleeping." Learning to take care of oneself includes rest time. Bedtime routines are important as a way to assist toddlers to wind down and relax in preparation for sleep. Routines can be associated with going to bed and caring for self.

ACTIVITY: Encourage children to pretend to put baby dolls to bed. Ask them, "What do you need to do first? What's next?" Provide dramatic play materials that represent objects associated with bedtime, such as blankets, stuffed animals, bottle or water glass, toothbrush, washcloth and soap, pacifier, cradle, and of course a bedtime storybook. Pretend with the children if they have trouble developing their own pretend scenario. With practice they will learn to engage in pretend play.

MATERIALS: baby dolls, stuffed animals, blankets, cradle, bottles, bath supplies, book, etc.

Calm-Down Time (Elizabeth Verdick)
AGE RANGE: 12–24 MONTHS
Respect (RT-4), Self-Discipline (SD-2, SD-3)

CHARACTER-RELATED CONTENT: This board book has sharp, colorful illustrations and rhyming text. Children enjoy reading and rereading this book. It puts words to feelings and provides a systematic method for calming oneself that toddlers can practice. Young children are learning about their feelings but may have difficulty managing them. This book gives ideas for managing emotions.

ACTIVITY: Model some of the techniques from the story, such as deep breathing or retreating to a quiet place. Since most toddlers have limited language, modeling actions that help us calm down may be more useful than talking about it, but also use language to explain. You might model for them, "I'm unhappy. I'm going to my cozy corner." Another example would be, "I'm mad. I need to stop and take a great big breath of air."

While children are calm, lead them in practicing the techniques. Say, "When I clap my hands, we take a deep breath and relax. Ready?" Clap hands, and model the deep breathing.

MATERIALS: none needed

Jump, Frog, Jump! (Robert Kalan)
AGE RANGE: 15–24+ MONTHS
Respect (RT-2)

CHARACTER-RELATED CONTENT: *Jump, Frog, Jump!* is a story about a frog who jumps from one problem to the next, but with a happy ending. This book uses the phrase "Jump, frog, jump," which children enjoy repeating at the right time when they listen closely. Books with predictable text present a great opportunity to work on listening skills.

ACTIVITY: As you read the words, pause before reading the repetitive phrase and give toddlers time to speak the anticipated phrase, "Jump, frog, jump." This requires children to listen attentively to the story so they know when to repeat the special words. Add to the fun by having the children make frog stick puppets out of construction paper and craft sticks to use when you read the book. Another activity that can be used with this book is a game of jumping lily pads. Cut out lily pads from art foam and stick them to the floor with tape. Children "jump" from lily pad to lily pad as they pretend to be the frog escaping from danger.

MATERIALS: construction paper, craft sticks, art foam, and tape

I Love You Through and Through (Bernadette Rossetti-Shustak)
AGE RANGE: 12–24 MONTHS
Caring (C-2)

CHARACTER-RELATED CONTENT: Toddlers learn from our love for them how to show affection and caring for others. This book shows all the ways we can love someone—top, bottom, inside, outside, happy side, sad side, silly side and mad side, eyes, ears, nose, toes . . . Nothing children do changes our loving care for them.

ACTIVITY: As you read the words, demonstrate all the ways you love a child by giving a one-finger kiss on the spot you love—eyes, mouth, ears, nose, hair . . . Toddlers may be able to model the one-finger kiss using a doll or stuffed animal. Show how to kiss your finger and then apply the kiss.

MATERIALS: doll or stuffed animal

Thank You Bear (Greg Foley)
AGE RANGE: 12–24 MONTHS
Caring (C-2), Integrity (I-4), Respect (RT-3)

CHARACTER-RELATED CONTENT: Bear found a little box and thought it was the "greatest thing ever" for Mouse. Bear showed the box to other animal friends—Monkey, Owl, Elephant—and others who did not admire it. Bear is almost discouraged, but then Mouse comes along. Mouse examines the box carefully and says it is the "greatest thing ever! Thank you Bear!" Bear demonstrates caring and courage in the face of adversity during his adventure with the box. Mouse demonstrates good manners when thanking Bear.

ACTIVITY: Toddlers love to use everyday boxes in their play. They are inexpensive toys that help children explore the concepts of over, under, inside, and outside. Provide a variety of different sizes of boxes for toddlers' play. Be nearby as they play, using words to describe the activity you see. Your encouragement and support while allowing independent play will make this experience the "greatest thing ever!"

MATERIALS: several boxes of different sizes and open space to play

Owl Babies (Martin Waddell)
AGE RANGE: 12–24 MONTHS
Caring (C-1, C-2, C-3), Honesty (H-1), Integrity (I-1)

CHARACTER-RELATED CONTENT: *Owl Babies* is a small board book with detailed pictures of three owl babies and their mother. The mother leaves, and the three babies are left to wonder about what she is doing and whether she will come back. Engaging text and the repeated theme of "I want my mommy!" will interest toddlers, who often experience these same feelings. Mother owl eventually comes back, and the babies are relieved and happy. Sharing feelings of missing a caregiver is an important issue for toddlers. The predicted return, despite feelings of worry and concern during an absence, re-creates and reinforces caring, honesty, and integrity for young children.

ACTIVITY: Make collages depicting baby animals and their parents. Prepare ahead of time by cutting out pictures of animal babies and parents, for example, dogs and puppies, pigs and piglets, cows and calves, and so on. Allow children to use glue sticks to glue pictures on paper to create a picture of animal babies and their parents. Toddlers enjoy the challenge of working with glue sticks, and you can use language to describe the animals and their babies, emphasizing the caring, consistent nature of these relationships.

MATERIALS: cut-out pictures of animal babies and parents, glue sticks, paper

Only You (Rosemary Wells)
AGE RANGE: 12–24 MONTHS
Caring (C-2), Integrity (I-1), Respect (RT-2, RT-5)

CHARACTER-RELATED CONTENT: Mother and Little Bear are beautifully illustrated doing activities together in this short book for toddlers. "Only you" refers to how Little Bear feels about his relationship with Mother Bear. Pictures show her close to Little Bear, encouraging independence and at the same time maintaining physical closeness and watchfulness. Little Bear helps, plays, waits, and cuddles with Mother Bear. The pages are sturdy, and the book includes tips for reading to toddlers and ways to extend learning. A conclusion is included for caregivers that recognizes the importance of relationships and one-on-one time with children under three years. Characteristics of caring, honesty, integrity, and respect are themes in this charming book.

ACTIVITY: Revisit the illustration showing Little Bear standing on a chair at the kitchen table and stirring some food in a bowl while Mother Bear supervises. Discuss what Little Bear and Mother are doing, then initiate a simple cooking project with your toddler, such as making brownies from a mix or making a salad or gelatin. Toddlers can easily stir and pour in premeasured ingredients. Wash hands as you begin and end the activity. Use smocks or aprons. You could also initiate other activities depicted in the book with your toddler, such as a close cuddling time while reading a good book or sharing a snack.

MATERIALS: recipe and ingredients for cooking project, cooking utensils such as bowls and spoons, smock or apron

Character-Building Activities for Two-Year-Olds

The activities in this chapter are designed for children ages twenty-four to thirty-six months. As in chapters 5 and 6, each activity includes the character trait(s) and the specific objective(s) supported, using the codes found at the end of chapter 4. A brief description of the character connection and materials needed, if any, is also provided.

The two-year-old year is typically a rewarding time in which to support character development. Most two-year-olds have developed significant vocabularies and abilities to think flexibly and creatively, skills that distinctly support and enhance their engagement in character-building activities. Most two-year-olds also have a solid awareness of self in relation to others and are beginning to consistently grasp that others have unique feelings and perspectives. They are often highly observant and quick to imitate behaviors and actions they see. Above all, two-year-olds' delightful and contagious excitement and curiosity about everything makes working with them both fun and rewarding. Caregivers of two-year-olds can usually begin to see the first fruits of their efforts in teaching and encouraging skills and character development.

Yet, as with teaching all ages and in all areas, it is important to be sensitive to the developmental stages and abilities of children as you plan and carry out your activities. Children progress at their own unique pace and follow individual trajectories in developing skills, interests, and strengths. Keep in mind the individual needs and abilities of every child while you select the activities that are most appropriate.

Be a Good Neighbor
AGE RANGE: 24–36 MONTHS
Respect (RT-5), Caring (C-2)

DESCRIPTION: When possible, bring young children along as you volunteer in your community or give assistance to friends and neighbors. Even though children aren't always skilled enough to provide actual "help," seeing adults engaged in helping others as a normal activity forms impressions and plants seeds of caring in them. Volunteer activities that are well suited for children to join include the following:

- Delivering clothing or household donations to a friend or neighbor or to a collection site. Young children can participate in sorting and folding clothing in advance. You can also talk to them about the satisfaction of passing along outgrown items to someone else who can enjoy them.

- Shopping for items to give to food banks, children's hospitals, or charitable fundraising events. Again, two-year-olds may not fully comprehend the whole picture, but seeing this as a normal occurrence can plant the seeds of valuing this type of generosity.

- Raking leaves for an elderly neighbor. Twos can't help effectively with this process, but they can nonetheless have their own child-size rake and be encouraged to go through the motions, feeling part of a joint family or group effort to help someone.

- Baking a treat to share with someone. Cooking is fun for two-year-olds, and they like to share their treats with others. They can begin to help with the process by putting premeasured ingredients in a bowl or stirring the contents.

- Visiting homes for the elderly to sing, share, or visit. Twos may be shy about visiting the elderly, but if they have a song or gift to share, they are more likely to enjoy participating. Carrying a baked treat or fruit to an elderly person is a meaningful gesture.

MATERIALS: vary depending on activity chosen

Character connection: Children learn and form impressions of caring through observing the behaviors and actions of the key adults in their lives. Making a point to include children when you volunteer or provide assistance to neighbors or your community is a powerful way to normalize volunteerism and caring in their little minds.

A Grown-Up's Memory Box
AGE RANGE: 24–36 MONTHS
Caring (C-1, C-2), Respect (RT-2, RT-4)

DESCRIPTION: Create a memory box containing nonfragile mementos and photographs from your past that can be used to spark conversation with two-year-olds and promote their listening skills and learning to show interest in another person. Make a point of including items in the box that trigger stories and memories to which they can relate, for example, your first baby shoe, a favorite childhood book or toy, or photographs of you with a beloved childhood pet, dressed up for trick-or-treating, blowing out birthday candles, or playing a game that the child might recognize, such as Duck, Duck, Goose. Sit down with the children and pick out a single object at a time from the box, using it as the spark for telling some brief story or memory from your childhood. For example, "When I was little, my favorite game was Duck, Duck, Goose. I remember we played it at my five-year-old birthday party."

MATERIALS: box, photographs or mementos from caregiver's past

Character connection: Children are naturally fascinated by adults' childhood and youth stories. Asking others about themselves and listening to their stories and memories is a way of showing respect and caring. A memory box facilitates rich opportunities for two-year-olds to practice respectful listening. Sharing your stories and memories with children also helps them to better know and understand you. Sharing stories from the memory box on a regular basis can become a very special bonding ritual.

A Child's Memory Box
AGE RANGE: 24–36 MONTHS
Caring (C-1, C-2), Respect (RT-2, RT-4)

DESCRIPTION: Create a memory box for a child. Place a few significant objects from the child's life into a solid, easy-to-open box, and label it with their name and birth date. For example, a parent might include a lock of hair from a first haircut, a picture of revealing a first tooth, first baby booties, or images of baby footprints. A child care provider might include a photo from the child's first day at the program, a significant piece of artwork, the crown or candle from a child's birthday celebration, or a sample piece from a child's favorite type of toy. When you take out the box, remove one item at a time, and use it as a "story starter" with either you or the child telling the story associated with the item, encouraging the child to share or ask questions. You can also ask questions or elaborate on his story to expand his vocabulary associated with an item.

Store the box in a special place out of reach so it's not available for daily play. Instead, take it out from time to time as a special event, letting it be the springboard for calm and focused sessions celebrating the child's life, memories, and unique attributes. After a showing and sharing of the child's memory box, put the items back, and store the box away again until the next time. Selectively add special items as time passes. Resist the temptation to put every possible thing in the box, as that could take away from the significance of each item.

MATERIALS: box, photographs or items that are special from the child's life

Character connection: Two-year-olds love hearing stories about themselves, not to mention receiving focused and undivided attention from their significant adults. This activity allows the adult to demonstrate—and the child to experience—unmistakable caring actions through the telling and celebrating of their unique stories and memories. This activity helps caregivers and children appreciate and honor milestones and progress. Respectful listening and celebrating your special moments together fuel warm, caring relationships.

Sharing Daily Highlights
AGE RANGE: 24–36 MONTHS
Caring (C-1, C-2, C-3), Respect (RT-1, RT-3), Self-Discipline (SD-2)

DESCRIPTION: Mealtimes provide many opportunities for creating rituals and practicing caring and respectful behaviors. Create a mealtime ritual by having each person at the table share a highlight from the day so far. You can initiate the activity with a question: "What has made you feel happiest today?" You may need to provide gentle coaching to help two-year-olds think of a highlight, such as, "What about when you made the beautiful picture of your dog, Toby?" or "I think you had your favorite waffles for breakfast this morning, didn't you?" You may also need to coach them on the idea of picking one or two happy events to share. Keep your reminders positive and model the sharing yourself, simplifying your own daily highlight so that it is comprehensible to a two-year-old. Encourage everyone at the table to listen respectfully and attentively to one another while others share. Once everyone has shared, acknowledge a feel- ing of gratitude, "Wow! I'm so happy for all the great things that have happened for each of us today!"

MATERIALS: none needed

Character connection: Meals are a time for interaction and relationship building. During mealtime, we have an opportunity to model caring and respect for others. Young children learn about respectful listening when they see us practicing it. Involving them in conversations about the good things that have happened each day helps them cultivate positive feelings and develop self-control and respect in listening to others. This activity may be quite brief and simple when children are two, but it can become the basis for a ritual that they can continue and value with parents and friends into and through their adulthood.

Play with Goop

AGE RANGE: 24–36 MONTHS

Integrity (I-4), Self-Discipline (SD-1, SD-2)

DESCRIPTION: Create a fun and interesting "goop" out of cornstarch and water.

Recipe:

Mix 3 cups cornstarch with 2 cups warm water. Gradually add the water and mix with your hands. It is done when it changes to a satiny texture.

You can add food coloring in with the water if you would like a variety of colors. The mixture is smooth and will run and drip through your fingers but also feel solid. Put a small amount of the goop in a plastic tub for each child present. Invite children to explore the goop with their hands. At first, they may be reluctant to put their hands in the unusual slippery mixture. Encourage them by demonstrating how you can put your hand in and move the mixture. Once they get over the strange feel, they will enjoy manipulating the goop. After the activity, have children wash and dry their hands thoroughly. If this is your first time making goop, mix up a batch ahead of time so that you understand the properties of the substance. You can vary the activity by providing implements, such as spoons or craft sticks, small toys such as cars or trucks, or measuring spoons and cups to use in the goop.

MATERIALS: smocks, plastic tubs, cornstarch, water, food coloring, spoons, craft sticks, and small toys

Character connection: Building confidence is an important step in facing new experiences with courage. If children have had success practicing skills in a safe environment, they will be more confident for new activities and new situations. Some young children are very reluctant to touch or play with slippery or slimy-feeling materials. This activity can help them become more adventurous. Manipulating the goop mixture also promotes finger strength and dexterity. Experimenting with goop and exploring different ways to handle and play with it can invite problem solving and self-control.

Setting the Table, Part Two

AGE RANGE: 24–36 MONTHS

Responsibility (RB-2), Caring (C-1, C-2, C-3)

(building on "Setting the Table, Part One" in chapter 6)

DESCRIPTION: Create a special place mat to help two-year-olds set the table. On a rectangular piece of construction paper, draw the shapes of each item in a table setting in their appropriate location: plate, spoon, fork, and napkin. Laminate the place mat for more durability. Lay the place mat on the table and let children "work the puzzle" by placing tableware in the correct spots.

Twos can also help with simple table-setting tasks, such as putting out salt and pepper, salad dressing, or condiments. Keep an eye out for simple food preparation activities they could also help with, such as tearing lettuce for a salad. Encourage children in their efforts, and praise them explicitly for their participation, saying, "You set out all the napkins. Thank you for being such a good helper."

MATERIALS: construction paper, markers, laminating film, place mats, plates, spoons, forks, and napkins

Character connection: Children can feel empowered by the experience of providing real help. They experience the pride that comes with taking responsibility and completing a task. The experience of chipping in to a group effort is also a powerful experience of caring. Even if the job isn't done as quickly or expertly as a parent or caregiver could do it, the child's lesson in cooperation and helping is too valuable to skip. Many chores can be broken down into small actions that young children can complete successfully. Even if they are not able to do the entire job, having some small responsibility helps the child feel like a valuable working member of the family or group, helping take care of self, others, and the environment.

Making My Bed
AGE RANGE: 30–36 MONTHS
Responsibility (RB-2)

DESCRIPTION: Two-year-olds may not be able to make their own beds, but they can learn to appreciate and participate in the process in simple, limited ways. Make it the two-year-old's job to fluff and arrange the pillows on her bed after an adult has straightened and folded the blankets. Let the child decide how the pillows get arranged, or rearranged, each day. Or at a child care center, two-year-olds can be assigned the task of putting away their naptime mats, blankets, and pillows.

MATERIALS: pillows, bed, nap mats, blankets

Character connection: Allowing children to complete as much of a task as they are capable of doing gives them opportunities to grow their skills. Accepting responsibility for completing tasks helps two-year-olds feel like they are valuable members of the family or group, capable of doing their share of the job.

Children's Car Wash
AGE RANGE: 24–36 MONTHS
Responsibility (RB-2), Caring (C-1, C-2, C-3)

DESCRIPTION: On a warm, sunny day, hold a "car wash" to clean children's outdoor riding toys. Alternatively, you could wash the real car or both the toys and the car in the same process. Give the child a small bucket with soapy water and a sponge. Assign the two-year-old a specific and realistic job, such as scrubbing the seats on the riding toys or the car's tires. Be sure the child is dressed appropriately, because clothing will get wet. This is a great way to have some fun on a hot summer day.

MATERIALS: bucket, scrub brush, sponge, soap, water, water-appropriate clothing

👥 Character connection: Making work fun helps children learn to complete jobs. The task may not be completed as efficiently as an adult would do it, but the gains for the young child are in learning to accept responsibility, finishing a job, and finding joy in successfully completing a task that helps others and the environment.

My Own Cleaning Potion
AGE RANGE: 24–36 MONTHS
Responsibility (RB-2)

DESCRIPTION: Make your own nontoxic cleaning spray and provide the two-year-olds with their own personal bottle of it to use in cleaning. You can find numerous simple recipes for nontoxic cleaning spray in books or online. For example, here is a simple mixture:

- 2 cups water

- 1 cup of white distilled vinegar

- a few drops of an essential oil for scent (available for purchase at many natural food stores)

Mix the first two ingredients and pour mixture into a spray bottle. Then offer children the choice between two different yet mild and pleasant scents, for example, lemon or lavender. Invite them to explore the scents by dipping the end of a cotton swab in the oil and passing it under their noses. Once the child chooses "her scent," you can add a few drops of her chosen oil to her cleaning bottle, and voilà! You have created her own personal cleaning solution. Make a colorful label for the cleaning spray bottle so she can recognize it. You could also prepare a child's own personal lightweight bucket with her own spray bottle, rags, and dust cloths.

Praise children for their efforts when they participate to any extent in cleaning. Encourage them to notice any results, such as when a table becomes clean or spots are removed from a surface they have cleaned.

MATERIALS: nontoxic cleaning spray ingredients (water, white vinegar, essential oil), spray bottle, lightweight plastic bucket, rags

Character connection: Giving children the opportunity to choose the scent for their own personal cleaning spray will help them to feel a sense of ownership, as well as responsibility for using it when the time comes for cleaning chores. Select those chores at which they can easily be successful, such as cleaning windows, baseboards, and surfaces that are at their level. Having a job helps children learn about responsibility and taking pride in a job well done.

Taking Care of Books
AGE RANGE: 24–36 MONTHS
Caring (C-3)

DESCRIPTION: Create a personalized book of reminders to help two-year-olds learn how to care for books. Take pictures of a child respecting the following rules:

- Use clean hands when you hold a book (picture of a child washing hands).

- Sit when you read a book (picture of a child sitting on a chair with an open book).

- Turn pages slowly and carefully (picture of a child carefully turning pages).

- Put books back on the shelf when you finish (picture of a child putting book on the shelf).

Place the pictures together in book form and add it to the bookshelf. Children will enjoy reading a book that includes their own pictures showing others how to follow the rules of caring for books.

MATERIALS: photo album or construction paper and laminating film, photos of children following book rules

Character connection: Books are fun, but they can also be damaged or torn. Like any possession, it is important to learn to take good care of them. Caring for books is a wonderful first lesson in caring for possessions and the home or child care environment.

WOW Time!
AGE RANGE: 24–36 MONTHS
Honesty (H-1), Integrity (I-3)

DESCRIPTION: Show special attention to and appreciation for two-year-olds when they do something that demonstrates trustworthiness. Receiving special positive feedback from adults affirms their choice and fuels their motivation to repeat the behavior. For example, you can call attention to a child's honesty by saying something like this: "Wow! Annie, thank you for giving Katelyn's toy back to her when you found it. Look how happy that made Katelyn feel."

This activity is also effective in the home setting when your two-year-old gives you an accurate description of an incident. If your child says, "I drop cup. It broke." You can respond with "Wow! Jesse, thank you for telling me exactly what happened. Accidents happen, but I need to know about them so I can help clean up the broken pieces." You can also make a point of describing and praising a child's honesty to other family members, perhaps even grand- parents. They will appreciate the recognition and feel proud and encouraged by it.

MATERIALS: none needed

Character connection: Thanking and praising children for trustworthy behaviors helps them recognize their importance and encourages their honesty.

The Building Process
AGE RANGE: 24–36 MONTHS
Self-Discipline (SD-1)

DESCRIPTION: Take photos to document a child's process of building a block tower. Photograph each stage, starting with the foundation layer. Take another picture as the tower gets taller. As he is working, praise the process more than the completion of the final tower. Later, show him the pictures that validate and celebrate the process. You might say, "Ethan, you worked so hard when you were making that tower. It took a long time, and you never gave up. That was awesome!"

You can expand on this activity by taking pictures of a house as it is being built or by taking children to watch a new building going up in the neighborhood. Talk about how the building process has many steps and uses a variety of tools, equipment, and machines.

MATERIALS: enough blocks to build tall towers, camera

Character connection: Learning to persist through longer projects is an important part of self-discipline. We can encourage two-year-olds to develop self-discipline by noticing and praising their persistence and patience with extended projects, as opposed to focusing primarily on their final outcomes.

Outdoor Painting
AGE RANGE: 24–36 MONTHS
Caring (C-3), Self-Discipline (SD-1)

DESCRIPTION: Open a large cardboard box so that it lies flat on the ground. Provide buckets with child-friendly water-based paint but no paintbrushes. Send children on a scavenger hunt outside to find something in nature to use as a paintbrush. There is no wrong answer to this problem. You will see children get creative painting with leaves, branches, rocks, sticks, and flowers. If an insect crawls across the painting, it becomes an artist also. The value in the process of painting exceeds the product, but children will enjoy their art experience.

MATERIALS: large piece of cardboard, water-based paints, buckets, clothing appropriate for painting

Character connection: Enjoying the outdoors comes naturally for children. Playing outdoors by definition supports exploration and creativity because it allows children to move about with greater freedom. This activity presents a problem-solving challenge in an outdoor setting, promoting exploration and creativity. It also facilitates confidence because there is no wrong way to handle the activity.

Hitting Hurts
AGE RANGE: 24–36 MONTHS
Caring (C-2), Respect (RT-4), Self-Discipline (SD-2, SD-3)

DESCRIPTION: Make a collage with pictures showing things you can hit and things you cannot hit. Select and cut appropriate pictures ahead of time and then sit down with children to go through them and sort into groups: "hit" and "no hit." Paste pictures on two sides of a large poster board or on two pieces of paper and post for future conversations. For example, pictures could include the following:

- Things You Can Hit: balls, pile of leaves, punching bag, balloons, pillows

- Things You Cannot Hit: people, animals, furniture, toys

Alternatively you could place each picture on an index card and sort cards into two baskets, one for things you can hit and one for things you cannot hit.

MATERIALS: magazine pictures, poster board or paper, glue, index cards, baskets for sorting

Character connection: Self-discipline develops progressively as children mature and begin to see others' perspectives. We can support them in their efforts toward self-discipline by giving them opportunities to identify, understand, and accept the thinking of others. This is an important step for two-year-olds and can help them develop empathy and respect for others, which will in turn help them control their impulsive nature to hit.

Feelings Song
AGE RANGE: 24–36 MONTHS
Caring (C-1), Respect (RT-4), Self-Discipline (SD-1, SD-2, SD-3)

DESCRIPTION: Sing the easy and often favorite song "If You're Happy and You Know It, Clap Your Hands." Encourage children to demonstrate the various emotions and actions mentioned.

Verses could include the following:

If you're happy and you know it,
   clap and smile.
If you're happy and you know it,
   clap and smile.
If you're happy and you know it,
   then your face will surely show it
   (*smile big*).
If you're happy and you know it,
   clap and smile.
If you're angry and you know it,
   growl with me.
If you're angry and you know it,
   growl with me.
If you're angry and you know it,
   then your face will surely show it.
If you're angry and you know it,
   growl with me.

If you're sad and you know it,
   go boohoo.
If you're sad and you know it,
   go boohoo.
If you're sad and you know it,
   then your face will surely show it.
If you're sad and you know it,
   go boohoo.

Other verses:

disappointed, go "Oh me!"
surprised, go "Wow!"

MATERIALS: none needed

Character connection: Two-year-olds may need help in identifying their feelings and emotions. They feel many emotions but often don't have language to describe them, leading to frustration. Caring for self includes understanding the emotions one experiences and learning to express them constructively and respectfully. This is an important stepping-stone to understanding and respecting others' feelings as well. This song can help children identify their own feelings and honor the feelings of others.

Talking about Feelings
AGE RANGE: 30–36 MONTHS
Caring (C-1), Respect (RT-4), Self-Discipline (SD-1, SD-2, SD-3)

DESCRIPTION: Gather a set of images from magazines depicting people showing different emotions. Guide two-year-olds to glue the pictures on paper and talk about the expressions depicted. Ask, "How do you think that person is feeling? Why do you think he is feeling sad?" If the child has difficulty verbalizing his answers, share some examples, such as, "Sometimes when I'm mad, I want to stomp my feet or look mean. What do you do to show you're mad?"

You could also make a book showing the different faces and emotions the children represent. You can take pictures of them expressing their emotions, such as happy, sad, angry, silly, and surprised.

Help young children understand emotions by using language to identify and describe their feelings. For example, Drew was disappointed, pouting when Daddy said, "No, you can't go outside. It's raining." When he began to pout, Daddy responded to his emotional expressions by using descriptive terms. "I see by your look that you're disappointed. I know you are disap-

pointed because I see your sad face and lower lip sticking out."

MATERIALS: pictures of children, paper, glue, clips to bind the book, magazines, scissors

Character connection: Learning how to identify feelings and emotions in themselves and in others is difficult for young children and requires practice. Caregivers can help children learn these skills by pointing out the physical signs that are evidence of a person's feelings. This helps two-year-olds learn to identify emotions, understand appropriate responses, and practice those responses in a nonthreatening environment.

Facing My Fears
AGE RANGE: 24–36 MONTHS
Integrity (I-4), Honesty (H-2)

DESCRIPTION: Use pretend play to act out young children's fears. For example, if a two-year-old is fearful of going to the doctor, initiate a pretend play scenario of a doctor visit. Or if a child fears a monster under the bed, plan a "monster hunt" and search high and low under beds and in closets, illuminating dark areas with a flashlight. Provide a night-light to help the child see at night or tell a story about a funny monster that makes you giggle and chases away all the other monsters.

MATERIALS: vary depending on scenario

Character connection: Two-year-olds are beginning to develop their imaginations and abilities to predict, but with those skills sometimes come fears. Those fears can be very real, even if children have difficulty explaining them. Acknowledge their fears, talk about them, and offer support in facing them. Being able to express and face fears with courage builds integrity and helps two-year-olds understand the difference between real and pretend.

Reading Together
AGE RANGE: 24–36 MONTHS
Respect (RT-5)

DESCRIPTION: Help children develop good listening skills during group reading time by providing friendly, positive nonverbal reminders. Make a sign with pictures on each side illustrating respect for reading time. On one side, show a child sitting quietly and on the other show a picture of some ears. Keep the sign handy when you start to read a book. The two reminders are to sit quietly and listen carefully.

MATERIALS: paper, paint stir stick, glue, pictures

Character connection: Listening to books in groups involves showing respect to others so that the book can be enjoyed by all. This can be challenging at times for two-year-olds. Nonverbal reminders can be helpful for reminding children of expectations without interrupting the reading process.

Seeing Instructions
AGE RANGE: 24–36 MONTHS
Respect (RT-2)

DESCRIPTION: Create picture cards for the instructions you find yourself repeating most often, such as "Sit," "Listen," "Be quiet," "Put your head down on your pillow," "Keep your hands in your lap," and so on. For each instruction, find a picture that portrays the concept. For example, use an image of someone looking through binoculars to portray the instruction "Look at me." Or use a picture of a mouse to illustrate the instruction "Be still and quiet like a mouse." Put the images on index cards, and put the cards on a loose-leaf ring, which you can carry in your pocket. Then on a regular basis, hold up a card to convey an instruction in place of stating it. Make sure to include some instruction cards that are just for fun, such as "Run in place," "Make a silly face," or "Clap your hands."

Spend time preparing two-year-olds for the visual instruction by playing a game. Flash the card and have the children act out the instruction. Explain that when you use the card, they do the action without talking. Play the game often so children will remember how to play. Next time you are reading a book and a child is disruptive, use the visual instruction card to remind the child of the rules. You do not interrupt your reading to children, and you quietly help the disruptive child refocus.

MATERIALS: index cards, glue, pictures of directions, loose-leaf ring

Character connection: Learning to listen, pay attention, and follow rules are all ways we show respect for others. You can help children learn and remember rules by keeping them simple and by making a game out of rule reminders.

Perk Up Your Ears
AGE RANGE: 24–36 MONTHS
Respect (RT-2)

DESCRIPTION: Record a variety of normal sounds that children can easily hear inside the house, in their child care, or in their normal outdoor environments. Be sure to record sounds repetitively or include at least ten to fifteen seconds of a continuous sound so as to allow enough opportunity for identification. Also be sure to document the sounds yourself so that you have a clear list for your own reference. Indoor sounds might include water running, doorbell, kitchen appliances, baby crying, people talking, and telephone ringing. Outdoor sounds could include birds singing, crickets chirping, traffic sounds, garbage trucks, dogs barking, a verbal walk indicator at a crosswalk, and children playing.

Once you have created a recording, gather children for a listening time. Start by indicating with a finger over your lips that it is time to be quiet and listen. Play a single sound from your recording and invite children to place their cupped hands behind their ears in a listening sign when they can identify the sound. For a more advanced level, invite children to group the sounds into categories, for example, human, animal, and machine, or loud and soft.

MATERIALS: recorder, notebook, pencil

Character connection: Listening is an important skill for children to be successful academically and socially. Children who listen are more apt to make friends and keep them. Learning to listen takes practice, but you can support this developing skill by modeling good listening and providing opportunities for two-year-olds to focus their listening skills through games and activities that require listening for success.

The Problem/Solution Jar
AGE RANGE: 28–36 MONTHS
Self-Discipline (SD-1, SD-2)

DESCRIPTION: On slips of paper, write brief scenarios depicting normal, everyday problems that two-year-olds might encounter at home or child care. Put the slips in a nonbreakable jar. During circle time or conversation time, initiate a discussion about problem solving. Let the child pick a scenario slip from the jar and hand it to you to read. Ask the child(ren) to suggest solutions for the problem.

These are some scenarios for the Problem/Solution Jar:

- There is only one truck, and two children want to play. What will we do?

- Betsy spilled her milk, and it made a puddle on the floor. What will we do?

- John wants candy, but Mommy says no. What will he do?

- Ainsley wants to go outside, but it's raining. What will she do?

You can use this activity when you have an unexpected wait. It's helpful to acknowledge when children are struggling with waiting time by saying, "Waiting is hard, but let's play a game while we wait." Some of the solutions they choose may not be wise choices, but this opens up the possibility for discussing consequences of "bad" choices.

If you need a more portable version of this game that will fit in your purse or bag, use a small empty tin with a hinged lid. Fold up the situations, and have them ready for the waiting time when you need to redirect or distract the children.

MATERIALS: plastic jar or small tin container, strips of paper with common problems

👥 **Character connection:** Young children experience problems daily and are learning how to solve those difficulties. Providing them with opportunities to think about problems in a nonthreatening environment helps them find solutions before they experience complications, giving them ideas for steps to follow.

Harry Head
AGE RANGE: 30–36 MONTHS
Caring (C-1), Integrity (I-4)

DESCRIPTION: Prepare for the activity by drawing a simple face with eyes, nose, ears, and mouth on a Styrofoam cup or small plastic planter. Have the children fill the cup to the rim with potting soil and sprinkle about a teaspoon of bluegrass seed on top. (Use a bluegrass variety of seeds, as it grows quickly and produces a type of grass that is relatively easy to cut.) Water the seeds regularly and place the cup on a sunny windowsill. In a few days, the bluegrass will begin to grow, and "Harry" will have a full head of grass-green hair that grows straight up and then parts in the middle. When Harry's hair is several inches long, allow your two-year-olds to cut the "hair" with safety scissors. This may require some assistance from an adult, as children may not have the coordination needed for scissor skills or are just beginning to develop this skill. You might consider purchasing some beginner's scissors, which require a fisted squeezing motion by the child in order to operate. This activity helps promote scissor skills because there is no wrong cutting—any snips are a success. With two-year-olds who simply aren't able to manage scissors well

enough to do their own cutting, invite them to watch an adult do it and to provide instructions about how they would like their Harry's hair to be cut. Continue to water regularly, and you can cut Harry's hair often. You might want to teach the following poem.

Harry Head
On Harry's head the grass seed goes,
Let him sit in the sun and watch his hair grow.
Add a little water, and some tender, loving care,
Before too long, you can cut Harry's hair.

MATERIALS: Styrofoam cup or small plastic container, markers, potting soil, bluegrass seed, safety scissors

👥 **Character connection:** All young children at some point will experience a haircut. This is a typical experience in self-care. However, sometimes children are fearful of getting their hair cut. This activity helps children learn about keeping hair neat while helping them face fears with courage by talking about the process and pretending.

Walking the Line
AGE RANGE: 24–36 MONTHS
Integrity (I-4), Responsibility (RB-1)

DESCRIPTION: Twos have mastered walking, so challenge them with opportunities to try jumping, walking backward, or walking on a board or line. When inside, use ribbon or wide tape on the floor, or for a more challenging experience, use a four-foot-long two-by-four board lying flat on the floor. Lead children to "walk the line" as they follow you in a game of "follow the leader." Walk the line or board forward, backward, and sideways, and then jump the length. Innovative ways of moving provide new levels of excitement and challenge that are fun but also require some courage to attempt. When playing outside, you can often find elements in the environment that allow children to experiment with movement, such as a painted line, a plank, or a curb they can walk.

MATERIALS: wide tape or a four-foot-long two-by-four board

Character connection: Introducing new and more challenging ways of moving can build confidence and scaffold skills to a more advanced level. Two-year-olds experience satisfaction and a boost in confidence when they are able to succeed at new challenges. It is important for young children to set goals, but it takes courage to complete goals that stretch their abilities. Attempting to complete a goal is an indicator of integrity. Even if the child does not succeed the first time, the process builds confidence in the child's ability.

Something Is Missing
AGE RANGE: 24–36 MONTHS
Honesty (H-3)

DESCRIPTION: Show two-year-olds three to four items, such as a golf ball, crayons, a book, and sunglasses. Allow them time to study the items and talk about the names of the items displayed and how they are used. Have children close their eyes, and then remove one of the items. When they open their eyes again, ask if anyone knows which item is missing. You control the difficulty of this game by the number of objects displayed, adjusting the number of items upward as children become more observant. This game helps develop a child's memory of details.

MATERIALS: small items such as a cup, crayons, golf ball, doll shoe, fork

Character connection: This activity supports children in practicing their ability to remember details. Children often have problems or disagreements with others and want to tell an adult what happened. Sometimes telling the basic facts is difficult. Being able to recall details is an important step in developing honesty.

What Did I Do?

AGE RANGE: 24–36 MONTHS
Honesty (H-3)

DESCRIPTION: This activity encourages two-year-olds to observe things and talk about them accurately. Practice by doing an action and having the children tell you about the action in detail. It may be helpful to have them imitate the action also. You might say, "I can do it, can you?" For example, the leader can jump up and down and then ask a child to tell about it. "What did I do? Now do it with me." In the next step, let a child initiate an action for others to describe and imitate. Encourage memory skills by asking children to do the second step after repeating the first step in the sequence. Two-year-olds can usually sequence two to three simple movements by memory.

MATERIALS: none needed

Character connection: Learning to communicate effectively requires many skills, vocabulary, and comprehension. Efficient communication also entails the ability to describe a sequence of events accurately. Opportunities for children to use their descriptive language skills help them develop accuracy in communication.

Bear Hunt

AGE RANGE: 24–36 MONTHS
Integrity (I-1), Honesty (H-2)

DESCRIPTION: Games and stories that have repetitive patterns can help children learn the concept of predictability or reliability. The game or story always follows the same sequence of words and events. Bear Hunt is a childhood favorite that carries the child through a path in a repetitive, predictable way. It's fun and helps children remember the repetitive sequence of events. It may also address a child's fears, as he knows that a fearful situation ends the same way every time with the child being safe at home. As you repeat the words, children follow the hand motions.

> (*speak in a chanting voice*)
> Let's go on a bear hunt. (*pat knees with hands in a steady rhythm*)
> Let's go on a bear hunt.
> Let's go on a bear hunt.

> I see some tall, tall grass ahead, (*place hand over eyes to look in distance*)
> Some tall, tall grass ahead.
> Can't go over it. (*circle hand over imaginary grass*)
> Can't go under it. (*circle hand under imaginary grass*)
> Can't go around it. (*circle hand around imaginary grass*)
> Guess we have to go through it. (*hold grass aside and stomp feet through*)
> Let's go on a bear hunt. (*pat knees in a steady rhythm*)
> Let's go on a bear hunt.
> I see a deep, deep river ahead, (*place hand over eyes to look in distance*)
> A deep, deep river ahead.

Can't jump over it. (*jump hand over imaginary river*)

Can't dig under it. (*dig hand under imaginary river*)

Can't go around it. (*circle hand around imaginary river*)

Guess we have to swim through it. (*pretend to dive in and swim imaginary river*)

Let's go on a bear hunt. (*pat knees in a steady rhythm*)

Let's go on a bear hunt.

I see a dark, dark cave ahead, (*place hand over eyes to look in distance*)

A dark, dark cave ahead.

Can't fly over it. (*fly hands over imaginary cave*)

Can't go under it. (*circle hand under imaginary cave*)

Can't wait outside it. (*stop hands in front of imaginary cave*)

Guess we have to go in it. (*creep in cave with hands out to feel the dark*)

I smell something stinky. (*pinch nose*)

I feel something fuzzy. (*pretend to feel bear*)

I see two big eyes. (*circle fingers around eyes like glasses*)

What is it? (*show scared face*)

It's a bear! Let's get out of here! (*put hands up in fear*)

Run! Run! (*pat knees in a fast, steady rhythm*)

Out of the cave, (*run out of cave, hands out to feel the dark*)

Run! Run! (*pat knees in a fast, steady rhythm*)

Swim the river, (*pretend to dive in river and swim fast*)

Run! Run! (*pat knees in a fast, steady rhythm*)

Through the tall grass, (*hold grass aside to make path, stomp feet through*)

Run! Run! (*pat knees in a fast, steady rhythm*)

I see home again. (*pretend to open, close, and lock the door*)

Whew! Safe again! Home sweet home.

MATERIALS: none needed

👥 Character connection: Remembering details is easier when we play games and songs that require memorizing and sequencing details, doing things the same repeatedly. The ability to memorize and sequence events improves with practice. Also, understanding that pretend bears are not real and cannot hurt us may help children deal with fears about imaginary or pretend characters.

What Will Happen?
AGE RANGE: 24–36 MONTHS
Integrity (I-1)

DESCRIPTION: Demonstrate the reliability of gravity by setting up a simple inclined plane. Use a sturdy sheet of cardboard with the edges folded up to keep small objects from falling off the side. Prop one end of the board on an elevated surface and place the other end on the floor. Provide small cars and objects to roll down the incline, but before the first car goes down, ask children to predict what will happen to the cars and objects placed on the incline. After a few times down the incline, the children can see the same thing will happen every time given the same incline and toy. The downward movement is something you can depend on to be true. Encourage children to experiment by laying the cardboard on the floor, thus making it level. What does the ball or car do when you set it at one end of the level surface? Or you could raise your cardboard to make the incline steeper. Young children can also experiment with using different objects on the inclined plane, such as a square block (although keep in mind that even a block will likely fall downward if the plane is at a steep angle).

MATERIALS: sturdy sheet of cardboard (ideally three to four feet in length), small cars and other objects, such as blocks

Character connection: Two-year-olds' ability to understand and predict things that occur consistently gives them confidence and helps them understand the concept of consistency.

Two Little Blackbirds
AGE RANGE: 24–36 MONTHS
Self-Discipline (SD-1), Honesty (H-2)

DESCRIPTION: Invite children to act out this familiar song/poem about two little blackbirds as you say or sing the words. Ask them to choose or create an area to serve as the "hill." It could be two chairs with a blanket or towel over them or a bench wide enough for two to sit. Two children sit on the "hill" and "fly away" at the appropriate time. Demonstrate how to pretend to be blackbirds (flap arms like a bird).

> Two little blackbirds sitting on a hill.
> One named Jack and one named Jill.
> Fly away Jack. (*first blackbird flies off the hill*)
> Fly away Jill. (*second blackbird flies off the hill*)
> Come back Jack. (*first blackbird returns to hill*)
> Come back Jill. (second *blackbird returns to hill*)

> Two little blackbirds sitting on a hill.
> One named Jack and one named Jill.
> (sung to the tune of "Twinkle, Twinkle Little Star")

MATERIALS: none needed

Character connection: Pretend play is an extremely valuable avenue for children's learning. It challenges them to comprehend the distinction between fantasy and reality, as well as to see multiple perspectives, solve problems, and grasp symbolism. Most two-year-olds are just beginning to embrace and enjoy pretend play. Parents and caregivers can support twos' development in this area by providing specific scenarios and prompts that guide them in their engagement with fantasy learning.

Rest-Time Calming
AGE RANGE: 24–36 MONTHS
Caring (C-1), Self-Discipline (SD-2)

DESCRIPTION: At rest time, after children are lying down, give them directions to help them relax. Develop a rhyming or chanting style in your voice to soothe and relax. As you chant the instructions, children begin to follow your lead and relax.

> Walk your fingers around your face. Around, around, around they pace.
> Up to your nose, walk them again. Gently slide them down to your chin.
> Down to your belly, around and around, until your belly button is found.
> Walk both hands, down to your thighs, ending neatly by your sides.
> Gently, gently, close your fists. Squeeze fingers tight and don't resist.
> Relax your fingers and spread them wide. Gently lay them by your sides.
> Close your eyes, time to dream, of butterflies, clouds, and birds that sing.
> Feel your tummy go in and out. Breathe in, breathe out, in and out.

As you repeat the instructions, reduce the volume of your voice until you are down to a whisper. Keep the instructions rhythmic in nature. The steady rhythm of your soft voice will relax children and help them rest.

MATERIALS: none needed

Character connection: Learning methods to help calm, relax, or soothe oneself is part of self-care. Self-discipline also involves being able to control yourself and keep a positive attitude. Activities that provide concrete ways children can practice self-control help them gain confidence in their own ability to self-calm.

Deep Breathing
AGE RANGE: 24–36 MONTHS
Caring (C-1, C-2), Self-Discipline (SD-2, SD-3)

DESCRIPTION: Invite children to picture themselves like balloons filling up with air. When the "balloon" is full, slowly let the air out and sink to the floor. This activity is useful when children are becoming overstimulated. When you sense a child's voice and activity level are escalating, say, "Let's take a deep breath, be like a balloon. Hold it. Now, let it go out slowly." Deep breathing can interrupt the trajectory of escalating noise and energy.

MATERIALS: none needed

Character connection: Use deep breathing as a transition or calming technique. When an activity becomes intense or the noise level escalates, take a few minutes to take a deep breath and relax. Deep breathing helps young children change the direction of behaviors that result from tension and stress, such as anger and disagreements.

Apology Accepted

AGE RANGE: 24–36 MONTHS
Honesty (H-3), Respect (RT-4)

DESCRIPTION: Teach two-year-olds about apologizing by role-playing situations and allowing them to play the parts of the injured and the injuring party. This gives them an opportunity to use the vocabulary in a nonthreatening situation, before it is needed. You can facilitate role playing by describing simple scenarios and inviting children to pretend to be the characters. For example, you could tell a story about a teddy bear bumping into another teddy bear and knocking him over. You model the words that the first Teddy might say, such as, "Oh my, I am so sorry. I did not mean to knock you down. I will be more careful next time. May I help you get up?" Then the second Teddy might say, "Oh, it's okay. I know you didn't mean to bump into me."

Or you could tell a story using two puppets and a stack of blocks. The first puppet is building with the blocks and says, "My tower is so tall." The second puppet accidently bumps it and knocks the blocks over. "Oh my, you knocked my tower down, Owen." The other puppet says, "Tom, I'm so sorry. I didn't mean to knock your tower over. Let me help you build it again."

In general, we adults can help children learn to apologize by demonstrating the following behaviors consistently:

- When a child is hurt, first comfort the hurt child.

- Offer guidance with language for an apology: "Barrett, you hurt Reece. You can help him feel better by saying you're sorry." Help children understand the words used to express the feelings.

- Give extra attention to the injured party, and explain how sad you feel to see a child injured.

- Be prepared to accept the possibility a child will not apologize. A forced apology teaches the wrong lesson—it teaches a child to lie.

The other side of this issue is learning to accept an apology. Sometimes it's just as difficult to get a child to forgive as it is to encourage apologizing. If one child apologizes, you can help the other with language for accepting. Katie knocked Amy down as she ran to the door. Amy started screaming! Katie said, "I'm sorry," but Amy was still hurt and angry. A caregiver can say to Amy, "I know you are feeling hurt and angry, but Katie didn't mean to hurt you. Can you ask Katie to be more careful next time and you can still be friends?" Children can resolve conflicts and still be friends.

MATERIALS: vary depending on scenario

Character connection: Apologies are an important show of respect and honesty. Two-year-olds are still quite young to fully grasp the concept of an apology. Their language skills may still be quite limited. This activity helps teach the words and actions to use and the steps to take in apologizing. Even without fully understanding the concept, going through these motions can plant seeds for sincerely felt and expressed apologies later in childhood.

Character-Building Activities with Books for Twos

As mentioned, books can be an important avenue for teaching and supporting character development. Through hearing books read to them, observing illustrations, and talking about the stories, children can learn about the world and form impressions of good character. Books can expose two-year-olds to examples of caring, respect, self-discipline, and honesty. In addition, the time you spend reading with children is invaluable and communicates your love and care for them.

Choose books carefully, paying attention to children's developmental needs. Reading time should be a joy and not a chore. If the child totally loses interest, switch to a different book or end the story time. Keep your reading voice interesting and enthusiastic. Make story time about her enjoyment of reading and not about finishing a book.

The following is by no means a comprehensive list of books for sharing character lessons. There are many others, and wonderful new books are being written all the time. This is merely a sampling of books found to be valuable in character development, along with ideas for activities to use with each to help guide children's thoughts and understanding of values.

Dawdle Duckling (Toni Buzzeo)
AGE RANGE: 24–36 MONTHS
Caring (C-1), Integrity (I-2)

CHARACTER-RELATED CONTENT: This book is a tale of a young duckling who wanders away from his mother, preening, playing, and having a fun time dreaming. He disregards her instructions, making an unwise decision to go off on his own until he realizes the danger and quickly returns to her protection. This book illustrates the importance of making wise decisions in order to stay safe. This skill is an important part of learning to care for self.

ACTIVITY: After reading the book, initiate a discussion of duckling's choices and actions by placing rubber ducks in water and acting out the story. You can follow up with a counting activity to see how many ducks remain in the pool after one wanders away.

Two-year-olds can also retell the story by acting like ducks, making wings with bent arms and thumbs tucked into armpits. To help little ones feel like they are in character, they can even make duckbill headbands out of orange construction paper to wear, or they can wear sports visors with big eyes glued on. Caregivers may need to model the pretend behavior to show children how to play, but with a little encouragement, they will enjoy acting like ducks. Waddle like the baby ducks, using the phrase repeated in the book:

"Quack, Catch up!" (*flap your "wings"*)

MATERIALS: rubber ducks, small tub of water, orange construction paper, sports visors, and google eyes

Pete the Cat and His Four Groovy Buttons (Eric Litwin)
AGE RANGE: 24–36 MONTHS
Self-Discipline (SD-2)

CHARACTER-RELATED CONTENT: Pete the Cat, wearing his favorite shirt with four groovy buttons, loses his buttons one at a time, but does he let that upset him? "Goodness, no!" He keeps on singing and maintains a positive attitude. Most two-year-olds get easily upset when they lose something. Some even have tantrums, unsure of how to deal with their feelings of disappointment. Two-year-olds can relate to Pete's situation, but Pete demonstrates a more constructive alternative to acting out disappointment using self-control to maintain a positive attitude.

ACTIVITY: Talk about the feelings you experience when you lose something important. Sing the song in the book as a chant. "Did Pete cry? Goodness, no! Buttons come and buttons go." A positive attitude is a choice, and we are responsible for our choices! Pete provides a fun role model.

Expand on the book with a counting activity using buttons (be sure the buttons are not a choking hazard by attaching them to something). Prepare five small felt pieces in the shape of shirts. Sew four, three, two, one, and zero buttons securely on the shirts. Children can sequence the shirts with the story of Pete the cat.

This is also a good time to play "Pass the Button." Children sit in a circle and pass a large button from child to child as music plays. When the music stops, the child with the button stands up and sings, "The button, the button, I have the button!" Music starts again, and the game continues with everyone participating.

MATERIALS: felt, needle, thread, large buttons, recorded music

Clean-Up Time (Elizabeth Verdick)
AGE RANGE: 15–30 MONTHS
Caring (C-3), Responsibility (RB-1, RB-2)

CHARACTER-RELATED CONTENT: Cleaning a child's room is always a challenge, but this book gives helpful hints for getting the job done in a quick, fun way. Young children actively participate in the cleaning process, remembering to check the space for anything out of place. They finish with hugs and high fives.

ACTIVITY: Make cleanup a game. Pretend to be busy bees working to clean the room. Concentrate on one area of the room at a time, working like a busy bee to get the job done. Work quickly, and celebrate with a cheer when the area is completed. Then fly (with arms outstretched) to the next area and repeat the process. Award children with a "BEE-utiful" bee award. You might have a special "buzzy bee" hug or celebrate with a "busy bee" dance when the child finishes a job. Make it special.

Note: Verdick has many books, all of which are helpful for character development. Here are some you may find helpful:

- *Listening Time* (Verdick 2008)
- *Mealtime* (Verdick 2011)
- *Naptime* (Verdick 2008)
- *On-the-Go Time* (Verdick 2011)
- *Sharing Time* (Verdick 2009)

MATERIALS: none needed

How Much Is That Doggie in the Window? (Iza Trapani)
AGE RANGE: 24–36 MONTHS
Caring (C-2)

CHARACTER-RELATED CONTENT: This is a rhyming book about a little boy who is saving his money to buy a puppy. When his family has needs, he spends his money on them instead of buying the puppy for himself. Without enough money, he is disappointed as he returns to the pet store and learns that the puppy is gone. When he gets home, he finds his parents have a surprise for him. This book teaches about caring for others in your family by doing simple things.

ACTIVITY: After reading the story, ask how the little boy spent his money. What did he do to show his family how much he cared for them? What did his parents do to show they cared? Talk about ways we show family members we care for them. Make a gift for someone in your life to show you care.

Make hot chocolate mix as a gift for a friend or family member. This recipe makes about eight cups of mixture. After preparing the mixture, divide into small ziplock bags or clean baby food jars, which can be decorated and given as gifts. Because all the ingredients are dry, it is easy for two-year-olds to help measure and stir.

Mix together:

6½ cups powdered milk

1 (5-ounce) package noninstant chocolate pudding mix

1 cup powdered chocolate drink mix

½ cup powdered nondairy creamer

½ cup confectioners' sugar

½ cup unsweetened cocoa powder

In a large bowl, combine all of the ingredients. Divide the mixture into the gift containers. Seal and decorate as desired. Store in a dry area for up to three months. Attach a tag with the following instructions: Hot Cocoa—Dissolve ⅓ cup cocoa mix in 1 cup boiling water.

MATERIALS: powdered milk, noninstant chocolate pudding mix, powdered chocolate drink mix, nondairy creamer, confectioners' sugar, cocoa powder, baggies or jars, decorations

No, David! (David Shannon)
AGE RANGE: 24–36 MONTHS
Integrity (I-2), Responsibility (RB-3)

CHARACTER-RELATED CONTENT: Children identify with David's problems as he makes one bad choice after another. He writes on the walls, tracks mud in the house, makes a mess in the tub, plays with his food, and jumps on the bed. He is in trouble! Does his mother still love him? The limited text is easy for children to memorize, and they will be "reading" the story with you as they learn about consequences for bad choices.

ACTIVITY: Writing on the wall is an activity that can be acceptable if it is done the right way. Cover the wall with a paint drop cloth that puddles on the floor or a large plastic shower curtain. Provide paint in buckets and large paintbrushes or small paint rollers for an art experience that is acceptable to do on the wall. Don't forget to cover clothing with a smock.

MATERIALS: paint drop cloth or large plastic shower curtain, paint, buckets, paintbrushes, painting smock

Blue Sea (Robert Kalan)
AGE RANGE: 24–36 MONTHS
Self-Discipline (SD-1)

CHARACTER-RELATED CONTENT: Simple text paired with simple illustrations tell the story of a little fish in the big blue sea. He is in danger of being swallowed by the big fish but outsmarts them by swimming through small openings to a safe place. Two-year-olds are at an age when they begin to become more independent, making decisions that can be dangerous without supervision.

ACTIVITY: Line up chairs, and cover them with a sheet to create a tunnel large enough for a two-year-old to crawl through. Or you can collect large appliance boxes and open them on both ends to create a tunnel. Twos love to crawl through tunnels, and you can invite them to imagine being like the little fish swimming through small places to get away from the big fish.

Discuss places that twos should not go alone. "We don't need to leave the house without mommy." "When we're at the park, always keep close to me. It's my job to keep you safe." How did the little fish solve the problem of the big fish following him? He swam to a safe place where the big fish could not follow. "Where are our safe places?" Use this book as a way to talk about safety for children.

MATERIALS: chairs and sheet, or appliance boxes

From Head to Toe (Eric Carle)
AGE RANGE: 24–36 MONTHS
Caring (C-1), Integrity (I-4)

CHARACTER-RELATED CONTENT: Exercise and movement are key aspects of self-care. This book has a fun way of inspiring the reader to exercise by moving in fun and different ways. Some of the challenges are difficult for a two-year-old. It will take courage to try moving in new ways, and a can-do attitude to be successful. That can-do attitude is important in establishing the child's sense of integrity later.

ACTIVITY: While you read this book, invite children to stand and try the different ways of moving that are described. The movements start simple but evolve to more difficult actions that might challenge two-year-olds.

MATERIALS: none needed

No Hitting! (Karen Katz)
AGE RANGE: 18–36 MONTHS
Self-Discipline (SD-1, SD-2, SD-3), Respect (RT-1)

CHARACTER-RELATED CONTENT: This book helps toddlers and twos learn to say no to hitting, screaming, squeezing, and yelling. Limited text and colorful illustrations offer a fun and painless way to redirect young children toward more acceptable behavior, learning self-discipline and respect for others.

ACTIVITY: Pretend to cry and tell a story about someone hitting you. "My teddy bear hit me while I was playing with my dishes." Wait for the reaction. Continue with the story, "He took my dishes, and he hurt me!" Set the stage for children to relate to your problem. Use the language you want the children to learn. "I told him, 'No hitting!'" Ask children, "What should he have done?" Twos may not be able to tell you a good solution to this problem, but by talking, they will learn how you solved the problem. "I told my teddy bear to use his words when he wanted something. No hitting!" Talk about what you should do when someone hits you. You also need to discuss those times when you want to hit someone. Using words to solve disagreements is a great thing to do if you know what words to use. Give children the language to use in these situations. Practice through pretend play.

MATERIALS: none needed

Henry Helps with Dinner (Beth Bracken)
AGE RANGE: 24–26 MONTHS
Responsibility (RB-2), Caring (C-2)

CHARACTER-RELATED CONTENT: Everyone needs a job, including two-year-olds. Henry helps his family prepare a special meal—it's taco night. He assists with lots of jobs, from tearing lettuce to carrying things to the table, all jobs that show he is responsible and able to help his family.

ACTIVITY: Plan a taco meal, and let the two-year-olds participate, just as Henry did. Twos can do simple food preparation with supervision, and the togetherness time is valuable for building that feeling of cooperation and trust.

- Wash hands carefully.
- Allow twos to tear prewashed lettuce into bite-size pieces.
- Add chopped tomatoes and other optional prepared ingredients.
- Serve with taco shells prepared by adults. Children may eat salad as a side dish or spoon it inside the taco shells.
- Have twos sprinkle cheese on the tacos.

MATERIALS: lettuce, tomatoes, cheese, taco shells, meat, and other taco ingredients

Pig Takes a Bath (Michael Dahl)
AGE RANGE: 18–30 MONTHS
Caring (C–1)

CHARACTER-RELATED CONTENT: After playing in the mud, Little Pig learns to take a bath using soap and a washcloth. This big board book has colorful pictures and bathing instructions children will enjoy. Bathing oneself is an important part of self-care. Twos are beginning to learn how to perform this task with supervision.

ACTIVITY: During bath time, use verbal cues to teach the skills needed to perform tasks with minimal adult help. Although two-year-olds still need supervision in the tub, we sometimes do too much for them and don't let them take on responsibility for some of their own care.

In another activity, pretend to take a bath while singing "Rub-a-Dub-Dub." Pretend to put soap on a washcloth to start the process. As you sing the following words, do the actions:

> Rub-a-dub-dub, sitting in the tub,
> Dirt is seen, wash it clean,
> Starting with my face, and just in case,
> Check behind the ears, now no tears!
> Washing my tummy, makes it feel funny.
> Legs are next, knees are checked,
> Washing my feet, oh so neat.

MATERIALS: soap, washcloth, shampoo, and other bath-time supplies

When Someone Is Afraid (Valeri Gorbachev)
AGE RANGE: 24–36 MONTHS
Caring (C–1), Respect (R–4)

CHARACTER-RELATED CONTENT: This book uses simple text to describe how different animals respond to fear. But how does a little boy respond to fear? He calls his mommy and daddy! Two-year-olds are beginning to develop fears as their imaginations grow. Caring about self includes learning ways to handle our fears and those of others.

ACTIVITY: After reading about fear, talk to the children about their fears. It is usually not helpful to try to convince a two-year old that he has no reason to be afraid. But you can suggest some solutions that may be comforting. Ask children to tell you about scary things, then

problem solve by making a list of the things that help us feel safe.

- Loud noises: Put fingers in ears.
- Dark: Get a flashlight or blanket.
- Toilet flushing: Put the lid down.
- Bugs: Walk away; you're bigger.
- Dogs barking: Sit on Mommy's lap.

It may also be helpful to calmly explain why certain situations are not dangerous. For example, "That dog barking is behind a fence and cannot get out and hurt you. You are safe." Or you can help children become gradually more accustomed to a fearful object, such as the vacuum cleaner, by sitting with them in a nearby room while someone else vacuums. Understanding that fear is a normal developmental stage can help you support young children. Also keep in mind that most fears go away on their own as children mature. Give it some time, comforting twos with your presence and reassuring them with your words until they conquer their fears.

MATERIALS: none needed

The Doorbell Rang (Pat Hutchins)
AGE RANGE: 24–36 MONTHS
Respect (RT-5)

CHARACTER-RELATED CONTENT: Sharing is not always easy, but this funny book about a group of children who decide to share a plate of cookies is a great way to start explaining it. It demonstrates the importance of sharing with everyone.

ACTIVITY: After reading the book, bake some cookies together, dividing them evenly and sharing them with friends or family. An easy recipe for completely no-bake cookie treats is a good way to help children learn some new skills.

Easy Squeezy S'mores

- chocolate-covered graham crackers
- marshmallow crème
- sprinkles (optional)

Place crackers on a plate. Spread graham crackers with marshmallow crème using a plastic knife. Sprinkle with optional candy topping. Top each with another graham cracker, and squeeze together.

Most older two-year-olds can easily help with some or all stages of preparing this treat. If some crackers break, no problem, eat the mistakes. Make plenty to share, and have fun.

MATERIALS: chocolate-covered graham crackers, marshmallow crème, sprinkles, plates

Alphabetical Listing of Activities

Chapter 5: Character-Building Activities
for Infants and One-Year-Olds

Chapter 6: Character-Building Activities for Toddlers

Chapter 7: Character-Building Activities for Two-Year-Olds

Bibliography of Children's Literature

Babies = 0   Toddlers = 1   Twos = 2

AGE	PAGE	BOOK
0	67	Adler, Victoria. 2009. *All of Baby, Nose to Toes*. New York: Penguin Group.
1	90	Alborough, Jez. 2002. *Hug*. Cambridge, MA: Candlewick Press.
2	123	Bracken, Beth. 2012. *Henry Helps with Dinner*. Mankato, MN: Picture Window Books.
0	70	Brown, Margaret Wise. 1991. *Goodnight Moon*. New York: Harper Festival.
2	119	Buzzeo, Toni. 2003. *Dawdle Duckling*. New York: Penguin Group.
0	50	Carle, Eric. 1987. *The Very Hungry Caterpillar*. New York: Philomel Books.
2	122	———. 1997. *From Head to Toe*. New York: Harper Collins Publishers.
1	91	Dahl, Michael. 2012. *Penguin Says "Please."* Mankato, MN: Picture Window Books.
2	124	———. 2010. *Pig Takes a Bath*. Mankato, MN: Picture Window Books.
1	94	Foley, Greg. 2007. *Thank You Bear*. New York: Viking Press.
0	67	Gentieu, Penny. 1998. *Baby! Talk!* New York: Crown Publishers.
2	124	Gorbachev, Valeri. 2005. *When Someone Is Afraid*. New York: Star Bright Books.
2	125	Hutchins, Pat. 1986. *The Doorbell Rang*. New York: Greenwillow Books.
0	68	Intrater, Roberta Grobel. 2005. *ABC Look at Me*. New York: Penguin Group.
0	66	Isadora, Rachel. 2008. *Peekaboo Morning*. New York: G. P. Putnam's Sons.
2	122	Kalan, Robert. 1992. *Blue Sea*. New York: Greenwillow Books.
1	93	———. 1995. *Jump, Frog, Jump!* New York: Greenwillow Books.
1	90	Katz, Karen. 2002. *Excuse Me!* New York: Grosset & Dunlap.
1	91	———. 2002. *No Biting!* New York: Grosset & Dunlap.
2	123	———. 2004. *No Hitting!* New York: Grosset & Dunlap.

AGE	PAGE	BOOK
2	119	Litwin, Eric. 2012. *Pete the Cat and His Four Groovy Buttons*. New York: HarperCollins.
0	68	Miller, Margaret 1998. *Baby Faces*. New York: Simon & Schuster.
1	89	Porter-Gaylord, Laurel. 2004. *I Love My Daddy Because . . .* New York: Dutton Children's Books.
1	89	———. 2004. *I Love My Mommy Because . . .* New York: Dutton Children's Books.
1	93	Rossetti-Shustak, Bernadette. 2005. *I Love You Through and Through*. New York: Cartwheel Books.
2	121	Shannon, David. 1998. *No, David!* New York: Blue Sky Press.
0	69	Sollinger, Emily. 2001. *Kisses for Mommy!* New York: Grosset & Dunlap.
0	66	Spinelli, Eileen. 1998. *When Momma Comes Home Tonight*. New York: Simon & Schuster Books for Young Readers.
2	120	Trapani, Iza. 1997. *How Much Is That Doggie in the Window?* Watertown, MA: Charlesbridge.
1	92	Verdick, Elizabeth. 2010. *Bedtime*. Minneapolis: Free Spirit Publishing.
0	69	———. 2008. *Bye-Bye Time*. Minneapolis: Free Spirit Publishing.
1	92	———. 2010. *Calm-Down Time*. Minneapolis: Free Spirit Publishing.
2	120	———. 2008. *Clean-Up Time*. Minneapolis: Free Spirit Publishing.
2	120	———. 2008. *Listening Time*. Minneapolis: Free Spirit Publishing.
2	120	———. 2011. *Mealtime*. Minneapolis: Free Spirit Publishing.
2	120	———. 2008. *Naptime*. Minneapolis: Free Spirit Publishing.
2	120	———. 2011. *On-the-Go Time*. Minneapolis: Free Spirit Publishing.
2	120	———. 2009. *Sharing Time*. Minneapolis: Free Spirit Publishing.
1	94	Waddell, Martin. 1992. *Owl Babies*. Somerville, MA: Candlewick Press.
0	68	Walton, Rick. 2000. *My Two Hands, My Two Feet*. New York: Penguin Putman Books.
1	95	Wells, Rosemary. 2003. *Only You*. New York: Viking Press.

References

AAP (American Academy of Pediatrics). 2011. "SIDS and Other Sleep-Related Infant Deaths: Expansion of Recommendations for a Safe Infant Sleeping Environment." *Pediatrics* 128 (5): 1341–67. doi: 10.1542/peds.2011-2285.

Ainsworth, Mary D. Salter. 1979. "Infant-Mother Attachment." *American Psychologist* 34 (10): 932–37.

Amsterdam, Beulah. 1972. "Mirror Self-Image Reactions before Age Two." *Developmental Psychobiology* 5 (4): 297–305.

Bornstein, Marc H., and Martha E. Arterberry. 2003. "Recognition, Discrimination and Categorization of Smiling by 5-Month-Old Infants." *Developmental Science* 6 (5): 585–99.

Brooks, Rechele, and Andrew N. Meltzoff. 2005. "Development of Gaze Following and Its Relation to Language." *Developmental Science* 8 (6): 535–43.

Christakis, Dimitri A., Frederick J. Zimmerman, and Michelle M. Garrison. 2007. "Effect of Block Play on Language Acquisition and Attention in Toddlers." *Archives of Pediatric and Adolescent Medicine* 161 (10): 967–71.

DeCasper, Anthony J., and William P. Fifer. 1980. "Of Human Bonding: Newborns Prefer Their Mothers' Voices." *Science* 208 (4448): 1174–76.

Dondi, Marco, Francesca Simion, and Giovanna Caltran. 1999. "Can Newborns Discriminate between Their Own Cry and the Cry of Another Newborn Infant?" *Developmental Psychology* 35 (2): 418–26.

Erikson, Erik H. 1950. *Childhood and Society*. New York: Norton Press.

Gerry, David, Andrea Unrau, and Laurel J. Trainor. 2012. "Active Music Classes in Infancy Enhance Musical, Communicative and Social Development." *Developmental Science* 15 (3): 398–407. doi: 10.1111/j.1467-7687.2012.01142.x.

Gilligan, Carol. 1993. *In a Different Voice: Psychological Theory and Women's Development*. Cambridge, MA: Harvard University Press.

Kim, Geunyoung, and Keumjoo Kwak. 2011. "Uncertainty Matters: Impact of Stimulus Ambiguity on Infant Social Referencing." *Infant and Child Development* 20 (5): 449–63.

Kohlberg, Lawrence. 1976. "Moral Stages and Moralization: The Cognitive-Developmental Approach." In *Moral Development and Behavior: Theory, Research, and Social Issues*, edited by Thomas Lickona, 31–53. New York: Holt, Rinehart, and Winston.

Lewis, Michael. 2013. *The Rise of Consciousness and the Development of Emotional Life*. New York: Guilford Press.

Lewis, Michael, and Jeanne Brooks-Gunn. 1979. *Social Cognition and the Acquisition of Self*. New York: Plenum Press.

Marion, Marian. 1999. *Guidance of Young Children*. 5th ed. Upper Saddle River, NJ: Prentice Hall.

Meltzoff, Andrew N., and M. Keith Moore. 1983. "Newborn Infants Imitate Adult Facial Gestures." *Child Development* 54:702–9.

Messinger, Daniel S., Alan Fogel, and K. Laurie Dickson. 1999. "What's in a Smile?" *Developmental Psychology* 35 (3): 701–8.

Moon, Christine, Robin Panneton Cooper, and William P. Fifer. 1993. "Two-Day-Olds Prefer Their Native Language." *Infant Behavior and Development* 16 (4): 495–500.

Parten, Mildred. 1932. "Social Participation among Preschool Children." *Journal of Abnormal and Social Psychology* 27 (3): 243–69.

Piaget, Jean. 1932. *The Moral Judgment of the Child*. Translated by Marjorie Gabain. London: K. Paul, Trench, Trubner.

Shore, Rima. 1997. *Rethinking the Brain: New Insights into Early Development*. New York: Families and Work Institute.

Smith, Mark K. 1997. "Friedrich Froebel (Fröbel)." Infed. http://infed.org/mobi /fredrich- froebel-frobel.

Vygotsky, Lev S. 1986. *Thought and Language*. Translated by Alex Kozulin. Cambridge, MA: MIT Press.

Wadsworth, Barry J. 1996. *Piaget's Theory of Cognitive and Affective Development: Foundations of Constructivism*. 5th ed. White Plains, NY: Longman Publishers.

Walden, Tedra A., and Tamra A. Ogan. 1988. "The Development of Social Referencing." *Child Development* 59 (5): 1230–40.

Wilcox, Barbara M., and Frances L. Clayton. 1968. "Infant Visual Fixation on Motion Pictures of the Human Face." *Experimental Child Psychology* 6 (March): 22–32.

Witherington, David C., Joseph J. Campos, Jennifer A. Harriger, Cheryl Bryan, and Tessa Margett. 2010. "Emotion and Its Development in Infancy." In *The Wiley-Blackwell Handbook of Infant Development*, vol. 1, *Basic Research*, edited by Gavin Bremner and Theodore D. Wachs, 568–91. 2nd ed. New York: Wiley-Blackwell. doi: 10.1111/b.9781444332735.2010.00023.x.